THE COUPON
COOKBOOK™

THE COUPON

COOKBOOK™

Money-saving Coupons and Favorite Recipes

THE COOKBOOK THAT PAYS FOR ITSELF™

MARION JOYCE

McGRAW-HILL BOOK COMPANY
New York   St. Louis   San Francisco
Hamburg   Mexico   Toronto

1 2 3 4 5 6 7 8 9 D O C D O C 8 7 6 5 4

ISBN 0-07-033067-0

LIBRARY OF CONGRESS CATALOGING IN PUBLICATION DATA

Joyce, Marion.
The coupon cookbook.
1. Cookery.   2. Coupons (Retail trade)   3. Marketing
(Home economics)   I. Title.
TX652.J69 1984   641.5′52   83-25532
ISBN 0-07-033067-0

Acknowledgments

I wish to thank the following for permission to use their recipes and for their generosity in providing coupons for this cookbook.

Brand	Company
ARGO®-KINGSFORD'S® Corn Starch	BEST FOODS / U.S. CPC INTERNATIONAL, Inc.
EAGLE® Brand Sweetened Condensed Milk	BORDEN, INC.
OLD LONDON® Melba Rounds	BORDEN, INC.
CARNATION® Evaporated Milk	CARNATION COMPANY
CARNATION® Nonfat Dry Milk	CARNATION COMPANY
CARNATION Instant Breakfast	CARNATION COMPANY
CONTADINA® Stewed Tomatoes	CARNATION COMPANY
DOLE® Pineapple	CASTLE & COOKE, INC.
MINUTE MAID® 100% Pure Lemon Juice From Concentrate	COCA-COLA COMPANY
SWEET 'N LOW®	CUMBERLAND PACKING CO.
BUTTER BUDS®	CUMBERLAND PACKING CO.
DANNON Yogurt	DANNON COMPANY, INC.
DEL MONTE® Fruit	DEL MONTE CORPORATION
DEL MONTE® Vegetables	DEL MONTE CORPORATION
MINUTE® Brand Tapioca	GENERAL FOODS CORPORATION
BIRDS EYE® COOL WHIP® Whipped Topping	GENERAL FOODS CORPORATION
DREAM WHIP® Whipped Topping Mix	GENERAL FOODS CORPORATION
BAKER'S® ANGEL FLAKE® Coconut	GENERAL FOODS CORPORATION
JELL-O® Brand AMERICANA® Golden Egg Custard Mix	GENERAL FOODS CORPORATION
JELL-O® Brand AMERICANA® Rice Pudding	GENERAL FOODS CORPORATION
CALUMET® Baking Powder	GENERAL FOODS CORPORATION
JELL-O ® Brand Instant Pudding	GENERAL FOODS CORPORATION
BAKER'S® GERMAN'S® Sweet Chocolate	GENERAL FOODS CORPORATION
BAKER'S® Unsweetened Chocolate	GENERAL FOODS CORPORATION
BAKER'S® Semi-sweet Chocolate	GENERAL FOODS CORPORATION
CERTO® Fruit Pectin	GENERAL PECTIN MANUFACTURING CORP.

(Continued on next page)

SURE JELL® Fruit Pectin	GENERAL PECTIN MANUFACTURING CORP.
HEINZ CHILI SAUCE	H.J. HEINZ COMPANY
HEINZ SPECIALTY VINEGARS	H.J. HEINZ COMPANY
HEINZ WHITE or CIDER VINEGAR	H.J. HEINZ COMPANY
A.1. Steak Sauce	HEUBLEIN, INC.
ROMANOFF® Caviar	IROQUOIS GROCERY PRODUCTS
MAGIC MOUNTAIN® Herb Tea	IROQUOIS GROCERY PRODUCTS
G. B. RAFFETTO®	IROQUOIS GROCERY PRODUCTS
KLONDIKE Ice Cream Bars	ISALY ICE CREAM COMPANY
SARA LEE® Croissants	KITCHENS OF SARA LEE
SARA LEE® Pound Cake	KITCHENS OF SARA LEE
KNOX® Unflavored Gelatin	KNOX GELATIN, INC.
LENDER'S® Bagels	LENDER'S BAGEL BAKERY, INC.
LIBBY'S Solid Pack Pumpkin	LIBBY, McNEILL & LIBBY, INC.
TRISCUIT® Wafers	NABISCO BRANDS, INC.
WHEATSWORTH® Stone Ground Wheat Crackers	NABISCO BRANDS, INC.
RITZ® Crackers	NABISCO BRANDS, INC.
NILLA® Wafers	NABISCO BRANDS, INC.
FIG NEWTONS® Cookies	NABISCO BRANDS, INC.
OREO® Chocolate Sandwich Cookies	NABISCO BRANDS, INC.
SHREDDED WHEAT TOASTED WHEAT & RAISINS	NABISCO BRANDS, INC.
NABISCO® Pecan Shortbread Cookies	NABISCO BRANDS, INC.
WEIGHT WATCHERS™ Mayonnaise	NUTRITION INDUSTRIES Corporation
WEIGHT WATCHERS™ Cheese	NUTRITION INDUSTRIES Corporation
WEIGHT WATCHERS™ Margarine	NUTRITION INDUSTRIES Corporation
LOUIS RICH™ Cold Cuts	OSCAR MAYER FOODS CORP.
LOUIS RICH™ Fresh Turkey Parts	OSCAR MAYER FOODS CORP.
OSCAR MAYER® Braunschweiger	OSCAR MAYER FOODS CORP.
OSCAR MAYER® Hot Dogs	OSCAR MAYER FOODS CORP.
CLAUSSEN® Sauerkraut	OSCAR MAYER FOODS CORP.
CLAUSSEN® Pickles	OSCAR MAYER FOODS CORP.
B&M® Brick Oven Baked Beans	PET, INC.
HIGH POINT® Decaffeinated Coffee	PROCTER & GAMBLE
HERB-OX Instant Bouillon & Bouillon Cubes	PURE FOOD CO.
QUAKER® OATS	THE QUAKER OATS COMPANY
FRENCH'S® Specialty Potatoes	R. T. FRENCH CO.
CHEX® brand Cereal	RALSTON PURINA COMPANY
SARGENTO® Cheese	SARGENTO CHEESE CO., INC.
SUNSWEET® Pitted Prunes	SUNSWEET GROWERS, INC.
SUNSWEET® Prune Juice	SUNSWEET GROWERS, INC.
SUN-MAID® Fruit Bits	SUN-DIAMOND GROWERS of CALIFORNIA
SUN-MAID® Raisins	SUN-DIAMOND GROWERS OF CALIFORNIA
SUN-MAID® Apricots	SUN-DIAMOND GROWERS OF CALIFORNIA
LIPTON® Soup Mix	THOMAS J. LIPTON COMPANY
WALDEN FARMS REDUCED CALORIE SALAD DRESSING	W F I CORP.

Contents

Note to the Reader:

Every recipe has at least one ingredient for which there is a money-saving coupon provided in this book. Many recipes have several applicable coupons. There are coupons for recipe ingredients that are <u>underlined</u>.

Introduction

Dear Friends,

I dedicate this unique cookbook to you, whether you are a beginner or an experienced cook, for this cookbook gives:

- *Excellent kitchen-tested recipes*, from the kitchens of the best brands in the world, for cooks of all levels.

- *Money-saving coupons for ingredients in all recipes.*

- *Important cooking and shopping tips.*

The featured products included in these recipes are all commonly used brands, staples that every kitchen needs—or needs to replenish. The coupons and reliable recipes will make your life easier and save you time, energy, aggravation, and money.

No need for the busy homemaker or career person to worry about what to serve for dinner or about unexpected company dropping in. If you keep the staples featured here on hand, you will be able to use these recipes to prepare mouth-watering dishes, from appetizers through desserts, quickly and confidently.

Shop in stores that give "double coupons" and you can save even more money by using the coupons in this book. I offer recipes and coupons together here so that you won't have to go searching through all your old coupons to prepare these recipes. Every recipe in this book has at least one ingredient for which there is a money-saving coupon provided in the last section. Many recipes have several applicable coupons.

I thank the participating brands for caring enough for their consumers to help to make consumers' lives better by providing these favorite recipes and money-saving coupons.

Important note: Recipes have been tested and developed using the specific featured brands only. As brands may vary in quality, texture, consistency, and actual ingredients, for accurate and reliable results, these recipes should be prepared with the suggested brands.

Happy cooking,

Marion Joyce
President
The Coupon Cookbook, Inc.

Appetizers and Hors d'Oeuvres

CHICKEN CHEESE BALL

This is an easy-to-prepare hors d'oeuvre that looks very special. Serve it as a family snack while watching TV or at a party.

   1 (8-ounce) package cream cheese, softened

   ½ cup finely chopped cooked chicken

   2 tablespoons chopped pimiento

   1 teaspoon WYLER'S® Chicken-Flavor Instant Bouillon

   ½ cup coarsely chopped nuts or sunflower seeds

   OLD LONDON® Melba Rounds

In small bowl, combine all ingredients except nuts and Melba Rounds; mix well. Shape into a ball; roll in nuts to coat. Chill. Garnish as desired. Serve with Melba Rounds. Refrigerate leftovers. Makes 1 cheese ball.

CHEESE NUT ROLL

Add an air of festivity to any occasion with this excellent hors d'oeuvre.

 1 package (3 ounces) cream cheese, softened
 2 cups finely grated American or process sharp cheese (about ½ pound)
 ¼ cup **HEINZ** Chili Sauce
 ⅛ to ¼ teaspoon hot pepper sauce (optional)
 ½ cup chopped pecans

Beat cheeses together until creamy; blend in chili sauce and hot pepper sauce. Place cheese mixture on wax paper or plastic film; shape into a roll* (8 × 1½ inches); roll in pecans. Wrap roll; chill several hours or overnight. Allow roll to stand at room temperature about 10 minutes before serving. Serve with assorted crackers. Makes 1 cheese roll (about ¾ pound).

*If cheese mixture is too soft to shape into a roll, chill until firm enough to handle.

BACON BROILED STUFFED PRUNES

These are so good that guests will ask you for the recipe. They're easy and quick to make.

24 <u>SUNSWEET</u> Pitted Prunes
24 large DIAMOND® Walnut pieces
12 slices bacon

Stuff prunes with walnut pieces. Partially cook bacon (do not allow to crisp); drain and cut each slice in half crosswise. Roll a half slice bacon around each stuffed prune and secure with pick. Broil until bacon is crisp. Makes 24 stuffed prunes.

SHRIMP SPREAD

This is a party favorite you can enjoy on any occasion.

2 (8-ounce) packages cream cheese, softened
¼ cup REALEMON® Lemon Juice from Concentrate
1½ cups chopped cooked shrimp (½ pound cooked shrimp)
1 to 2 tablespoons finely chopped green onion
1 tablespoon prepared horseradish

1 teaspoon Worcestershire sauce

¼ teaspoon pepper

⅛ teaspoon garlic powder

OLD LONDON® Melba Toast

In small mixer bowl, beat cheese until fluffy; gradually beat in REALEMON.® Stir in remaining ingredients. Chill to blend flavors. Garnish as desired. Serve with OLD LONDON® Melba Toast. Refrigerate leftovers. Makes about 3 cups.

TRADITIONAL CHEX PARTY MIX

Originally developed in 1955! And so delicious and versatile, it's been a tradition ever since.

½ cup (1 stick) butter or margarine

1¼ teaspoons seasoned salt

4½ teaspoons Worcestershire sauce

2⅔ cups CORN CHEX cereal

2⅔ cups RICE CHEX cereal

2⅔ cups WHEAT CHEX cereal

1 cup salted mixed nuts

Preheat oven to 250° F. Heat butter in large shallow roasting pan (about 15 × 10 × 2 inches) in oven until melted. Remove. Stir in seasoned salt and Worcestershire sauce. Add CHEX brand cereal and nuts. Mix until all pieces are coated. Heat in oven 1 hour. Stir every 15 minutes. Spread on absorbent paper to cool. Makes about 9 cups.

Microwave directions: In a large bowl melt butter on high 1 minute. Stir in seasoned salt and Worcestershire sauce. Add CHEX and nuts. Mix until all pieces are coated. Microwave on high 6 to 7 minutes, stirring every 2 minutes.

Hot & Spicy Variation: Follow above recipe using 8-cup combination of your favorite CHEX cereals and add ½ teaspoon chili powder and ¼ teaspoon bottled hot pepper sauce. Follow cooking directions as above.

NEW CAVIAR PIE

This is an updated version of an extremely popular and elegant hors d'oeuvre that is easy to prepare. Surprisingly, it's easy on the pocketbook, too.

    1 large sweet onion, finely chopped

    6 hard-cooked eggs, chopped

    3 tablespoons mayonnaise

    1 package (8 ounces) cream cheese, softened

  ⅔ cup sour cream

    1 jar (3½ ounces) **ROMANOFF** Lumpfish Caviar (see note)

Drain chopped onion on paper toweling 30 minutes. Butter bottom and sides of 8-inch springform pan. In a bowl, combine eggs and mayonnaise. Spread in bottom of pan in even layer. Sprinkle with onion. Combine cream cheese and sour cream, beating until smooth. By the spoonful, drop onto onion. With wet table knife, spread gently to smooth. Cover. Chill 3 hours or overnight. A half-hour before party time, drain caviar (see note). Just before serving, distribute caviar on top of cream cheese layer. Run knife around sides of pan; loosen and lift off sides. If desired, garnish with lemon and parsley sprigs. Serve with small pieces of pumpernickel bread. Serves 10 to 12.

Note: Gently spoon lumpfish caviar onto several layers of paper toweling; drain about 30 minutes in refrigerator. For salmon caviar, open jar, and turn on its side to allow juices to run out.

CHERRY TOMATOES ROMANOFF

A no-cook hors d'oeuvre that is very simple to prepare and attractive to look at. Use economical types of caviar*.

    1 pint small cherry tomatoes
    ⅔ cup sour cream
    1 teaspoon chopped fresh dill or 1½
        teaspoons minced green onion
    2 tablespoons **ROMANOFF** Caviar

Wash 1 pint small cherry tomatoes; cut thin slice from bottom to make stand firmly. Cut thin slice from tops. With teaspoon, scoop out half of pulp. Drain upside down on paper toweling. Combine ⅔ cup sour cream with 1 teaspoon chopped fresh dill or 1½ teaspoons minced green onion. Spoon about ½ teaspoon into each tomato cavity. Top each with ¼ teaspoon ROMANOFF Caviar* using 2 tablespoons in all. Garnish with mini-sprig of dill. About 24.

*Use ROMANOFF Salmon, Black or Red Lumpfish, Whitefish or Golden Whitefish Caviar.

CAVIAR-STUFFED MUSHROOMS

For easy, elegant entertaining.

¾ cup salad oil

¼ cup cider vinegar

1 garlic clove, coarsely chopped

Dash freshly-ground black pepper

30 to 36 medium-size mushrooms

1 pkg. (8 ounces) cream cheese, softened

¼ cup mayonnaise

3 tablespoons minced onion

½ cup (4 ounces) **ROMANOFF Caviar**

In shallow bowl, combine oil, vinegar, garlic, and pepper. Wash and remove stems from mushrooms. Coat caps with dressing; set aside, hollow side up. Combine cheese with mayonnaise and onion. Fill mushrooms with cheese; top each with rounded ¼ teaspoon of caviar. Provide plates and forks. Makes 30 to 36 stuffed mushrooms.

BRAUNSCHWEIGER HOLIDAY DIP

This holiday dip can be shaped as a tree for Christmas, a turkey for Thanksgiving, or an egg for Easter.

2 packages (8 ounces each) <u>OSCAR MAYER</u>® Braunschweiger Liver Sausage

1 cup (8 ounces) sour cream or plain yogurt

2 teaspoons dill weed

<u>CLAUSSEN</u>® Kosher Pickle Slices

<u>CLAUSSEN</u>® Kosher Pickle Halves

Cherry tomatoes, olives, carrots, celery, and other fresh vegetables

Fresh chopped parsley

Combine Braunschweiger, sour cream, and dill in bowl; blend until smooth. Shape into a triangle on large tray or serving platter. Decorate with pickles, olives, and other vegetables to resemble Christmas tree. (The garland is made of pickle slices; the tree trunk is a pickle half.) Sprinkle with parsley. Use fresh vegetables and pickles to dip into tree. Makes 24 servings.

DILLY OF A DIP

This "dilly of a dip" is delicious with fresh vegetables. It's also good with fish or as a topping for baked potatoes.

1   cup (8 ounces) sour cream
¾   cup chopped **CLAUSSEN®** Kosher
     Pickle Slices (garlic-flavored)
2   tablespoons pickle brine
1   tablespoon chopped onion (optional)
¼   teaspoon dill weed

Combine ingredients; chill. Serve with fresh vegetable dippers (celery, carrots, cauliflower, broccoli), potato chips, or assorted snack crackers. Makes 1¾ cups.

EMERALD GREEN VEGETABLE DIP

1   cup washed spinach leaves
1   cup mayonnaise
3   ounces cream cheese
⅓   cup dry **CARNATION** Nonfat Dry Milk
¼   cup sliced green onion
1   tablespoon lemon juice
½   teaspoon Worcestershire sauce
¼   teaspoon salt
2   tablespoons water, if desired

Measure spinach leaves by pressing firmly into measuring cup. Place spinach, mayonnaise, cream cheese, dry nonfat dry milk, green onion, lemon juice, Worcestershire sauce, and salt in blender container. Process on medium speed, carefully pushing ingredients down sides with rubber scraper, until well blended. Add water for slightly thinner dip, if desired. Chill at least 2 hours. Stir before serving. Makes about 2 cups.

Suggested Dippers: Strips of zucchini, cucumber, carrot, celery, flowerettes of broccoli, cauliflower, mushrooms, cherry tomatoes, crackers, chips, cooked shrimp, chunks of chicken or ham.

COOKING TIP: Add CARNATION Nonfat Dry Milk in its dry form to this dip. High in protein and iron, this colorful dip will become a party favorite.

PEEK-A-BOO PICKLES

These make great appetizers and also go well with soups or salads. Try them anytime!

        Butter or margarine, softened
    8 slices white bread, crusts removed
    1 package (6 ounces) **OSCAR MAYER**®
       Smoked Cooked Ham
    8 slices process American cheese
    2 whole **CLAUSSEN**® Pickles, quartered
       lengthwise
    8 toothpicks

Spread bread slice with butter; top with one slice ham and one slice cheese. Place pickle spear diagonally across top of cheese, corner to corner. Fasten remaining corners over pickle spear with toothpicks. Place on greased baking sheet. Bake in 400° F oven 8 to 10 minutes or until cheese melts and bread is slightly toasted. Remove toothpicks. Serve hot. Makes 8 sandwiches.

Soups, Salads, Side Dishes— Vegetables, and Sauces

SOUPS

IMPERIAL SHRIMP BISQUE

Use Black or Red Lumpfish or Golden Whitefish **ROMAN-OFF** Caviar. They are very reasonably priced and make this a super special, elegant soup.

2 cans (13 ounces each) full-strength
  shrimp bisque
¼ cup cream
¼ cup dry sherry
  Sour cream
2 tablespoons **ROMANOFF Caviar**

Combine bisque and cream in saucepan. Bring just to boil, stirring often. Stir in sherry. Ladle into heated soup plates. Top each serving with a dollop of sour cream and a heaping teaspoon of caviar. Serves 4.

Note: Canned condensed cream of shrimp soup may also be used.

PILGRIM HARVEST SOUP

An easy recipe for a deliciously hearty soup.

- 1 package (2 to 3 pounds) <u>LOUIS RICH</u>™ <u>Turkey Wing Drumettes</u> or <u>Drumsticks</u>
- 6 cups water
- 2 tablespoons instant chicken bouillon
- 1 teaspoon poultry seasoning
- ¼ teaspoon black pepper
- 1 bag (1 pound) assorted frozen vegetables
- ¼ cup alphabet or tiny shell pasta

Combine turkey, 6 cups water, and seasonings in large saucepot. Bring to a boil; turn down heat. Cover. Simmer 2 hours. Remove turkey from bone. Bring turkey, vegetables, pasta, and broth to a boil; turn down heat. Cover. Simmer 10 minutes more. Makes 8 cups.

ONION CHEESE SOUP

You will enjoy this simple HERB-OX variation of this classic soup.

- 1 large onion, sliced thin
- ½ cup butter
- ¼ cup flour
- ½ teaspoon dry mustard

2 cups boiling water

4 packets **HERB-OX** Beef Flavored Instant
    Broth and Seasoning

1 quart milk

2 cups grated Cheddar cheese (½ pound)

Cook onion in butter in soup pot 5 minutes, until translucent, but not brown. Sprinkle with flour and mustard, stir. Gradually add boiling water. Cook over low heat, stirring, until mixture is smooth and thickened. Add instant broth, stir to dissolve. Cover pan, simmer 15 minutes, stirring often. Add milk, heat just to boiling point. Add cheese, stir until cheese melts. Makes 8 servings.

QUICK 'N' HEARTY SOUP

This can be a meal in itself. Serve with a salad and a delicious bread.

1½ pounds ground chuck

1¾ cups (14½-ounce can) **CONTADINA**
    Stewed Tomatoes

3 cups (three 8-ounce cans) CONTADINA
    Tomato Sauce

1¼ cups (10½-ounce can) beef broth

2 cups water

2 tablespoons instant minced onion

1 teaspoon garlic salt

1 teaspoon marjoram leaves

¼ teaspoon pepper

6 cups (24-ounce package) frozen
   vegetables for stew

Brown ground chuck in Dutch oven. Drain off excess fat. Add remaining ingredients; mix well. Heat to boiling. Reduce heat; boil gently, uncovered, 30 minutes or until vegetables are tender. Stir occasionally. Makes about 3 quarts.

BOUILLABAISSE

Here is CONTADINA Stewed Tomatoes' excellent version of bouillabaisse.

1 cup chopped onion

1 cup chopped celery

2 tablespoons salad oil

3⅓ cups (two 14½-ounce cans)
   CONTADINA Stewed Tomatoes

⅔ cup (6-ounce can) CONTADINA Tomato
   Paste

1½ cups water

1 crushed large garlic clove

1 teaspoon thyme leaves

1 teaspoon oregano leaves

1 teaspoon salt

¼ teaspoon pepper

1½ pounds fresh clams in shell

1½ pounds white fish

½ pound shelled, deveined raw shrimp

Sauté onion and celery in oil in 5-quart Dutch oven until tender. Add tomatoes, tomato paste, water, garlic, thyme, oregano, salt, and pepper. Break up tomatoes. Cover and simmer 30 minutes. Scrub clams under running water. Place in large saucepan. Add a half-inch boiling water. Cover and cook over medium heat until shells just open, about 5 minutes. Strain clam liquid through paper towels; reserve 1 cup. Keep clams warm. Cut fish into bite-size pieces. Add to tomato mixture. Cook until fish is almost done, about 10 to 15 minutes. Add shrimp; cook additional 5 minutes. Add reserved clam liquid and clams. Heat just to serving temperature. Makes 12 cups.

BROCCOLI SOUP

Using your blender or food processor makes this a quick-and-easy recipe. Perfect for any season, served hot or cold.

1 package (10 ounces) BIRDS EYE® Chopped Broccoli

1½ tablespoons MINUTE® Tapioca

1 teaspoon salt

Dash of pepper

2 cups milk

1 tablespoon finely chopped onion

2 tablespoons butter or margarine

Prepare broccoli as directed on package; drain, reserving liquid. Add water to liquid to make ½ cup. Keep broccoli warm. Combine tapioca, salt, pepper, milk, measured liquid, and onion in saucepan. Let stand 5 minutes. Cook and stir over medium heat until mixture comes to a boil.

Pour hot mixture and broccoli into blender or food processor. Blend at high speed for 2 minutes, or until smooth. Add butter. Serve hot or chilled. Makes about 3¾ cups or 4 servings.

Note: To prepare larger quantities, prepare each batch in blender separately.

SALADS

LITELINE SPINACH SALAD

This is a wholesome and delicious salad to serve for the figure-conscious guest.

    1 can (16 ounces) **DEL MONTE** Lite
       Sliced Pears
       Tarragon Dressing (see recipe)
    4 cups chopped fresh spinach
    1 cup sliced fresh mushrooms
    1 cup cherry tomatoes, halved
    1 cup alfalfa sprouts

  1 can (11 ounces) <u>DEL MONTE</u> Mandarin
     <u>Oranges</u>, drained

Drain pears, reserving liquid. Prepare Tarragon Dressing. Toss spinach with pears, mushrooms, tomatoes,
alfalfa sprouts, and oranges. Serve with Tarragon
Dressing. Makes 4 servings, 108 calories per serving.

TARRAGON DRESSING

     Liquid from pears
  2 tablespoons white wine vinegar
  1 teaspoon prepared mustard
  $\frac{1}{2}$ teaspoon salt
  $\frac{1}{4}$ teaspoon tarragon, crumbled

Thoroughly blend all ingredients.

MARINATED MUSHROOM SALAD

HEINZ Tarragon Vinegar adds just the right touch to this
salad. It's perfect for everyday family dinners or special dinners.

  $\frac{1}{2}$ cup <u>HEINZ</u> Tarragon Vinegar
  $\frac{1}{2}$ cup salad oil
  2 tablespoons minced parsley
  1 clove garlic, minced

½ teaspoon salt

½ pound fresh mushrooms, sliced (about
   2½ cups)

1 medium onion, sliced

Lettuce

2 hard-cooked eggs, quartered

Mayonnaise or salad dressing

Combine first 5 ingredients in jar; cover; shake vigorously. Pour dressing over mushrooms and onions; toss lightly to coat. Cover; marinate several hours, tossing occasionally. Drain; serve in individual lettuce-lined bowls; garnish with egg quarters and mayonnaise. Makes 4 servings (about 2¼ cups).

PEPPERMINT RASPBERRY SALAD

MAGIC MOUNTAIN® Herb Tea is the featured ingredient in this salad. Enjoy the unusual combination of the peppermint and raspberry.

1 package raspberry gelatin (3-ounce size)

2 cups boiling water

4 bags MAGIC MOUNTAIN® Peppermint
   Spice Herb Tea

1 8¼-ounce can crushed pineapple,
   drained

1 1-pound can pear halves, drained

Sour cream, optional

In bowl, dissolve raspberry gelatin in boiling water. Add
tea bags (remove tags), and steep five minutes. Remove
tea bags and stir in crushed pineapple. Let cool. In cake
pan, or jello mold, arrange pear halves, cut side up, in
spoke pattern. Pour gelatin mixture over and let set till
firm. Garnish with sour cream, if desired. Serves 5 to
6.

QUICKIE CAESAR SALAD

This is a quick version of an all-time favorite. You can use
lemon juice instead of heavy dressings to add flavor to salads,
especially when you are watching your weight.

$\frac{1}{2}$ cup salad oil

1 garlic pod (or "clove")

$\frac{1}{4}$ teaspoon dry mustard

1 beaten egg

1 tablespoon Worcestershire sauce

$\frac{1}{4}$ cup **MINUTE MAID®** Lemon Juice

$\frac{1}{2}$ teaspoon salt

$\frac{1}{2}$ teaspoon coarsely ground pepper

$\frac{1}{2}$ cup Parmesan cheese

1 head romaine lettuce, "deribbed" and
torn

1 cup croutons

2-ounce can flat anchovy fillets (optional)

Mash garlic and add to salad oil. Set aside. Mix mustard, egg, Worcestershire sauce, MINUTE MAID lemon

juice, salt, pepper, and Parmesan cheese in jar and shake well. Just before serving, place torn lettuce in wooden bowl. Strain oil over all. Add croutons and anchovies to salad. Pour jar mixture over all and toss well. Serves 4.

CREAMY PINEAPPLE BUFFET SALAD

A pretty and delicious addition to your buffet.

> 1 can (20 ounces) <u>DOLE Sliced Pineapple in Syrup</u>
>
> 1 cup water
>
> 1 package (3 ounces) lemon-flavored gelatin
>
> ¼ cup diced celery
>
> ¼ cup diced green onions
>
> ¼ cup diced cucumber, peeled, seeded
>
> 2 tablespoons prepared horseradish
>
> ½ pint whipping cream

Drain pineapple, reserving syrup. Stand pineapple slices along sides of a 6-cup ring mold. Boil 1 cup water; add to gelatin. Stir until dissolved. Add ¾ cup reserved syrup. Refrigerate until mixture is the consistency of unbeaten egg whites. Toss together celery, onions, cucumber, and horseradish. Fold into gelatin. Whip cream and fold into gelatin mixture. Pour mixture over pineapple slices into ring mold. Chill until firm. To unmold, carefully run a knife around edges. Place in a large pan of warm water for 10 seconds and invert on serving platter. Makes 10 servings.

SAUERKRAUT SALAD

Crisp, white Sauerkraut Salad is a tasty accompaniment to many meals. It has just 50 calories per serving when made with a low-cal sweetener.

1 jar (2 pounds) **CLAUSSEN®** Sauerkraut, drained

1 cup sugar*

1 cup white vinegar

3 stalks celery, chopped

2 medium green peppers, chopped

1 medium onion, chopped

½ can (16 ounces) pitted ripe olives, sliced

In large bowl combine all ingredients. Cover and chill several hours or overnight. Serves 8.

*To further reduce calories, an artificial sugar replacement can be substituted. Use as package directs for equivalency to granulated sugar or to taste.

LAYERED VEGETABLE SALAD

This colorful, attractive salad will enhance any table setting.

6 cups chopped iceberg lettuce

1 cup chopped red cabbage

1 cup chopped red onion

1 can (8 ounces) CHUN KING Sliced Water Chestnuts, drained

1 can (17 ounces) <u>DEL MONTE Sweet Peas (No Salt Added)</u>, drained

1 can (17 ounces) <u>DEL MONTE Whole Kernel Corn (No Salt Added)</u>, drained

2 cups shredded carrots

1 cup mayonnaise (no salt added)*

½ cup sour cream

2 tablespoons sugar (optional)

Place lettuce in 3-quart straight-sided dish or 13 × 9-inch serving dish. Top with layers of cabbage, onion, water chestnuts, peas, corn, and carrots. Combine mayonnaise with sour cream. Blend in sugar, if desired. Spread evenly over carrots. Cover tightly and refrigerate several hours for flavors to blend. Makes 10 servings.

*Reduced-calorie mayonnaise may be used.

SAVORY GREEN BEANS

The convenience of **DEL MONTE** canned vegetables makes it easy to prepare interesting and delicious vegetable dishes such as this year round.

3 slices bacon, diced

1 small onion, sliced

2 teaspoons corn starch

¼ teaspoon salt

¼ teaspoon dry mustard

1 can (16 ounces) <u>**DEL MONTE** Blue Lake Cut Green Beans</u>

1 tablespoon brown sugar

1 tablespoon vinegar

1 hard-cooked egg, chopped

Cook bacon until crisp; remove from skillet. Add onion to 1 tablespoon bacon drippings; cook until tender. Blend in corn starch, salt, and mustard. Drain beans, reserving ½ cup liquid. Stir in reserved liquid. Cook, stirring constantly, until thickened and translucent. Blend in sugar and vinegar. Add beans. Heat. Top with bacon and egg. Makes 4 servings.

GLAZED CARROTS

WEIGHT WATCHERS Margarine saves you calories in this recipe. These carrots are delicious as an accompaniment to other vegetable and meat dishes.

> 1 10-ounce package frozen crinkle-cut
>   carrots
> 2 tablespoons **WEIGHT WATCHERS**
>   Margarine
> ½ cup orange marmalade

Heat margarine and marmalade over moderate heat until melted. Mix glaze with cooked carrots. Serves 4.

Orange Carrots: Substitute orange juice for marmalade.

HARVARD CARROTS

Everyone will love these carrots. HEINZ Wine Vinegar gives them this special flavor. You can use vinegar to heighten the flavor of many vegetables.

2 cups thinly sliced carrots

1 cup water

3 tablespoons granulated sugar

2 teaspoons corn starch

½ teaspoon salt

3 tablespoons **HEINZ Wine Vinegar**

1 tablespoon butter or margarine

Cook carrots in water in covered saucepan just until tender. Drain, reserving ¼ cup cooking liquid. In saucepan, combine sugar, corn starch, and salt. Stir in vinegar and reserved liquid. Cook over low heat, stirring constantly, until thickened and clear. Stir in butter; add carrots; heat. Makes 3 to 4 servings (about 1⅔ cups).

BRAISED CUCUMBER AND CORN

When prepared in creative ways, as in this easy recipe, vegetables can become the highlight of a meal.

1 medium onion, chopped

2 tablespoons sweet butter

2 tablespoons flour

¼ teaspoon dill weed

⅛ teaspoon pepper

1 can (17 ounces) **DEL MONTE Whole Kernel Corn (No Salt Added)**

2 cups sliced cucumber, cut in half

Sauté onion in butter until tender. Stir in flour, dill, and pepper. Gradually add liquid from corn. Stir in cucumber, reduce heat; simmer, covered, 15 minutes. Add corn; heat through. Serves 6.

BAVARIAN KRAUT

Serve Bavarian Kraut with pork chops, ribs or Polish sausage . . . it's also great on hot dogs and bratwurst.

    1 package (8 ounces) OSCAR MAYER®
      Bacon
    2 medium onions, chopped
    1 pound fresh mushrooms, sliced
    1 jar (32 ounces) CLAUSSEN®
      Sauerkraut, drained

Cut bacon into 1-inch pieces. In Dutch oven, cook bacon and onion over medium-low heat until bacon is crisp and onions are tender. Add mushrooms and sauté about 5 minutes. Add sauerkraut, stirring occasionally until heated through. Serves 6.

WILTED LETTUCE

Surprised by the name of this recipe? Try it as a side dish or a salad. You'll love it either way.

      4 slices bacon
    ¼ cup HEINZ Apple Cider Vinegar
      1 teaspoon sugar
    ¼ teaspoon salt
      Dash pepper
  4–5 cups bite-size pieces leaf lettuce
      2 tablespoons chopped parsley (optional)
      2 tablespoons sliced green onion or
        minced onion

Sauté bacon until crisp. Drain bacon on absorbent paper; crumble; set aside. Cool skillet; stir vinegar and next 3 ingredients into bacon drippings; heat to boiling. Pour hot dressing over lettuce and remaining ingredients; toss. Garnish with crumbled bacon; serve immediately. Makes 4 servings (about 5 cups).

VEGETABLE FRIES

Zucchini, cauliflower, mushrooms, and onion rings are dipped in a thick batter and fried. The batter coats easily but cooks crisp. Sure to be a favorite at all your parties.

Coating:

  ½ cup flour*

  1 teaspoon onion salt

  ½ teaspoon ground oregano

  ¼ teaspoon garlic powder

  1 egg, slightly beaten

  ⅓ cup milk

  1 tablespoon vegetable oil

  5 cups **CORN CHEX** Cereal, crushed to

    1½ cups

  Hot oil for frying

Coating will cover:

3 medium unpeeled zucchini; cut each in half crosswise and then cut each half lengthwise into 8 wedges

or

1 pound fresh mushrooms, cleaned

or

1 pound cauliflower broken into flowerettes (5½ to 6 cups)

or

1 large onion, cut into ¼-inch slices and separated into rings (about 4 cups)

In medium bowl combine flour, salt, oregano, and garlic powder. Add egg, milk, and oil. Mix until smooth. Place CHEX brand cereal crumbs in large plastic food storage bag. If necessary, pat vegetables dry with paper toweling. Toss vegetables, a handful at a time, in batter; drain off excess. Place vegetable pieces in plastic bag. Shake to coat with crumbs. Place on cake rack. Let dry 10 minutes before frying. Drop from slotted spoon into 375° F oil. Fry zucchini, mushrooms, and cauliflower about 2 minutes; fry onions about 1½ minutes or until golden, turning to brown evenly. Drain on absorbent paper. Serve immediately. Makes 8 servings.

*Stir flour; then spoon into measuring cup.

BRAUNSCHWEIGER HERB STUFFING

This recipe makes enough for one 12-pound turkey or 6 to 8 Cornish game hens.

> 1 package (4 ounces) OSCAR MAYER® Braunschweiger Liver Sausage
>
> 1 package (6 ounces) chicken stuffing mix
>
> 1 medium onion, chopped
>
> 2 stalks celery, chopped
>
> ¼ cup butter
>
> 1½ cups hot water

Combine Braunschweiger, stuffing mix with seasoning packet, onion, celery, butter, and water in large bowl. Place stuffing in a 2-quart casserole dish. Bake in 350° F oven 30 minutes. Serves 6.

CHICKEN STUFFING

RITZ® Crackers make this stuffing especially delicious.

> ½ cup chopped onion
>
> ½ cup chopped celery
>
> 6 tablespoons BLUE BONNET® Margarine
>
> 1 (8-ounce) package RITZ® Crackers, crushed (about 1 quart)
>
> ½ cup PLANTERS® Walnuts, chopped

½ cup milk

1 egg, beaten

¼ cup snipped fresh parsley

1½ teaspoons poultry seasoning

⅛ teaspoon ground black pepper

In large skillet, over medium high heat, sauté onion and celery in BLUE BONNET Margarine until golden brown. Mix in remaining ingredients until well blended. Spoon into 1-quart casserole; bake at 350° F for 25 to 30 minutes. Makes about 3 cups.

SAUCES, SPREADS, AND DRESSINGS

RANCH SALAD DRESSING

A dieter's delight. This is a great salad dressing that is easy on the waistline because of WEIGHT WATCHERS Mayonnaise.

1 cup WEIGHT WATCHERS Mayonnaise

1 cup buttermilk

1 tablespoon dried parsley flakes

2 teaspoons instant minced onion

½ teaspoon salt (optional)

¼ teaspoon celery salt

¼ teaspoon garlic powder

Blend all ingredients with wire whisk until smooth. Refrigerate until serving. Keeps for several days in refrigerator. Yield: 2 cups.

BASIC GRAVY

Corn Starch makes gravy smooth, with no floury taste or whitish color.

2 tablespoons fat drippings

2 cups liquid (water, broth or bouillon)

2 tablespoons **ARGO®** or **KINGSFORD'S®**

   Corn Starch

¼ cup cold water

   Desired seasonings

Measure fat into roasting pan. Stir in liquid. Cook over medium heat, stirring to loosen browned particles. Remove from heat. Mix corn starch and water. Stir into pan. Add seasonings. Stirring constantly, bring to boil over medium heat. Boil 2 minutes. Makes 2 cups.

ARGO®, KINGSFORD'S® are registered trademarks of CPC International Inc.

BASIC SAUCES

These are no-fail, no-fuss sauces.

Medium White Sauce

1 cup cold milk

1 tablespoon **ARGO®** or **KINGSFORD'S®**
Corn Starch

2 tablespoons margarine

¼ teaspoon salt

⅛ teaspoon pepper

In saucepan, gradually stir milk into corn starch. Add margarine, salt and pepper. Stirring constantly, bring to boil over medium heat. Boil 1 minute. Makes 1 cup. (For creamed vegetables, poultry, meat or fish.)

Herb Sauce

Add ¼ teaspoon dried dill weed or basil to 1 cup Medium White Sauce.

Cheese Sauce

Stir 1 cup shredded cheese into 1 cup Medium White Sauce until cheese melts.

ARGO®, KINGSFORD'S® are registered trademarks of CPC International Inc.

WEIGHT WATCHERS GOLDEN SAUCE

The **WEIGHT WATCHERS** Cheese and Mayonnaise makes this so good that dieters won't mind counting calories. It's good for the rest of the family, too.

½ cup **WEIGHT WATCHERS Part-Skim Milk Cheese,** cubed

½ cup **WEIGHT WATCHERS** Mayonnaise

Dash dry mustard

Dash cayenne

Melt cheese in top of double boiler over medium heat. When melted, add remaining ingredients. Stir until smooth. Serve over hot turkey or chicken, over egg or tomato sandwiches. Excellent over hot cooked vegetables and in casseroles. Yield: 1 cup.

ALL-PURPOSE SWEET-SOUR SAUCE

Prune juice is a natural, nutritious sweetener for sauces. Once you start to use it in cooking, you'll want to do so frequently because it's so good.

⅓ cup apricot-pineapple preserves

2 tablespoons vinegar

1 tablespoon catsup

2 teaspoons soy sauce

1½ teaspoons corn starch

½ cup **SUNSWEET** Prune Juice

In a saucepan, combine all above ingredients except prune juice. Slowly stir prune juice into mixture and bring to a boil. Reduce heat and cook about 1 minute longer or until mixture thickens. Makes about ¾ cup.

FRUIT BITS SAUCE

This is a versatile recipe made with ingredients that should be in most homes.

2 tablespoons butter or margarine

¼ cup granulated sugar

⅛ teaspoon cinnamon

½ cup orange juice

½ cup **SUN-MAID** Fruit Bits

In a small saucepan, melt butter; add sugar, cinnamon, juice, and fruit bits. Bring to a boil; remove from heat. Serve warm over heated, folded crepes, pancakes, waffles, French toast, ice cream. Makes about 1 cup sauce.

ORANGE-GRAPEFRUIT JELLY

If you've never made your own jelly before, this is a great recipe to start with.

1 box **SURE-JELL®** Fruit Pectin
2¼ cups water
1 can (6 fluid ounces) frozen concentrated
    orange and grapefruit juice, thawed
3½ cups (1½ pounds) sugar

To make the jelly. Thoroughly mix fruit pectin, water, and concentrate in 6- or 8-quart saucepot. Place over high heat and stir until mixture comes to a full boil. Immediately add all sugar and stir. Bring to a *full rolling boil* and *boil hard 1 minute,* stirring constantly. Remove from heat and skim off foam with metal spoon. Ladle quickly into hot sterilized glasses. Cover at once with ⅛ inch hot paraffin. Makes about 4 cups or about 5 (8 fluid ounce) glasses.

GINGER MARMALADE

Marmalade lovers will savor this unique flavor.

3½ cups prepared fruit (3 medium oranges,
    1 medium lemon, 1½ cups water, and
    ⅛ teaspoon baking soda)
1 cup (about 6 ounces) chopped
    crystallized ginger

5 cups (2¼ pounds) sugar

1 pouch **CERTO®** Fruit Pectin

First prepare the fruit. Remove skins in quarters from 3 oranges and 1 lemon. Lay quarters flat; shave off and discard about half the white part. With a sharp knife or scissors, slice remaining rind very fine, or chop or grind. Place in saucepan; add 1½ cups water and ⅛ teaspoon baking soda. Bring to a boil, cover, and simmer 20 minutes. Section or chop peeled fruit; discard seeds. Add pulp and juice to rind, cover and simmer 10 minutes longer. Measure 3½ cups into 6- or 8-quart saucepot. Add ginger.

Then make the marmalade. Thoroughly mix sugar into fruit in saucepot. Place over high heat, *bring to a full rolling boil,* and *boil hard 1 minute,* stirring constantly. Remove from heat and at once stir in fruit pectin. Skim off foam with metal spoon. Ladle quickly into hot jars, filling to within ¼ inch of top. Cover and process in boiling water bath for 5 minutes. Makes about 6 cups or about 7 (8 fluid ounce) jars.

GRAPE BUTTER

Family and friends will enjoy the wonderful flavor of this special recipe.

3 cups prepared fruit (about 3 pounds fully ripe Concord grapes)

¼ teaspoon cinnamon

¼ teaspoon cloves

5¾ cups (2½ pounds) sugar

¾ cup water

1 box **SURE-JELL®** Fruit Pectin

First prepare the fruit. Thoroughly crush, one layer at a time, about 3 pounds grapes. Force crushed fruit through a food mill or press through a sieve. Measure 3 cups into large bowl or pan. Stir in spices.

Then make the butter. Thoroughly mix sugar into fruit; let stand 10 minutes. Mix water and fruit pectin in small saucepan. Bring to a boil and boil *1 minute*, stirring constantly. Stir into fruit. Continue stirring *3 minutes*. (A few sugar crystals will remain.) Ladle quickly into scalded containers. Cover at once with tight lids. Let stand at room temperature 24 hours; then store in freezer. Small amounts may be covered and stored in refrigerator up to 3 weeks. Makes about 9 cups or about 10 (8 fluid ounce) containers.

PINEAPPLE-STRAWBERRY JAM

This is simply scrumptious!

4 cups prepared fruit (1 medium fully ripe pineapple* and about 1 quart fully ripe strawberries)

7 cups (3 pounds) sugar

1 pouch **CERTO®** Fruit Pectin

First prepare the fruit. Pare 1 pineapple; grind or finely chop. Thoroughly crush, one layer at a time, about 1 quart strawberries. Combine fruits. Measure 4 cups into 6- or 8-quart saucepot.

Then make the jam. Thoroughly mix sugar into fruit in saucepot. Place over high heat, *bring to a full rolling boil* and *boil hard 1 minute,* stirring constantly. Remove from heat and at once stir in fruit pectin. Skim off foam with metal spoon. Ladle quickly into hot jars, filling to within ¼ inch of top. Cover and process in boiling water bath for 5 minutes. Makes about 8 cups or about 9 (8 fluid ounce) jars.

*Or use 1 can (20 ounces) crushed pineapple in syrup.

Main Dishes—
Meats, Poultry,
and Meatless
Dishes

A.1. STROGANOFF

This delicious favorite can be easily prepared for a special occasion.

- 1 pound boneless sirloin steak, cut in strips $1 \times \frac{1}{4} \times 2$ inches
- 2 tablespoons butter (or margarine)
  Salt and pepper
- $\frac{1}{2}$ cup chopped onion
- 1 medium clove garlic, minced
- $\frac{1}{2}$ pound fresh mushrooms, sliced
- 3 tablespoons A.1. Steak Sauce
- 4 teaspoons flour
- 1 cup beef broth
- 2 tablespoons white wine
- $\frac{1}{8}$ teaspoon dill weed
- $\frac{3}{4}$ cup sour cream

In skillet, quickly brown meat in butter. Lightly sprinkle with salt and pepper. Remove and keep warm. Cook onion, garlic, and mushrooms in drippings. Stir in A.1. and flour. Cook, stirring, over low heat for 2 minutes. Add broth and wine. Simmer, uncovered, 5 minutes. Mix in dill, sour cream, and beef strips. Just heat through. Serve over cooked noodles or rice, if desired. Serves 4 to 6.

BEEF ROULADEN

A favorite German dish made with crisp, crunchy CLAUSSEN pickles.

        6 slices OSCAR MAYER® Bacon
    2½ to 3 pounds round steak, cut ¼-inch
        thick
      ¼ cup Dijon mustard
        1 large onion, chopped
        3 CLAUSSEN® Kosher Dill Pickles, cut
        lengthwise into quarters
        2 tablespoons oil
        1 cup water
        1 teaspoon instant chicken bouillon
        1 can (8 ounces) tomato sauce
        1 bay leaf
      12 ounces medium noodles
        Toothpicks
        2 tablespoons flour
      ¼ cup water

Cut bacon slices in half. Trim steak, removing bone and excess fat. Divide into 12 pieces. Pound into approximately 8×4-inch pieces. Top each piece with 1 teaspoon mustard, 1 tablespoon onion, and ½ bacon slice. Lay pickle across narrow end of each piece. Roll up; secure with toothpicks. Brown meat in oil in large skillet. Add water, bouillon, tomato sauce, and bay leaf. Cover. Bring to a boil. Turn down heat. Simmer 1 to 1½ hours until tender. Cook noodles according to package directions; drain. Place on platter. Remove toothpicks from meat rolls; place on noodles. Cover to keep warm. Mix flour and water. Stir into sauce in skillet. Cook on medium, stirring constantly, until mixture thickens and boils. Serve with beef rolls and noodles. Serves 6.

STUFFED CABBAGE

Stuffed cabbage is always a favorite. Make it with **SWEET 'N LOW** and save on the calories.

2 medium-size onions, cut in chunks

1 large head cabbage

2 pounds lean ground veal or beef
Freshly ground pepper to taste

1 teaspoon garlic powder

2 cups tomato juice, divided

4 packets **SWEET 'N LOW**

2 tablespoons lemon juice

In large saucepan, cook onions and cabbage in boiling water about 5 minutes. Drain, leaving onions in saucepan and removing cabbage. Mix ground meat with pepper, garlic powder, and ½ cup tomato juice. Divide in 18 portions. Separate cabbage leaves and place a portion of meat on each. Roll up and fasten with toothpick. Place in saucepan with onions. Stir SWEET 'N LOW and lemon juice into remaining tomato juice. Pour over all. Cover and gently simmer 1 hour, or until cabbage is tender and meat is cooked through. Serves 18.

MEXICAN CASSEROLE

Mexican food is becoming ever more popular. Try this spicy casserole using TRISCUIT® Wafers. You'll love the results.

```
 1  pound lean ground beef
⅓  cup sliced onion
 1  (16-ounce) can tomato sauce
½  cup water
 1  (4-ounce) can chopped green chilies,
    drained
 2  to 3 teaspoons chili powder
½  teaspoon salt
 1  (15-ounce) container ricotta cheese
 1  egg
 4  ounces Cheddar cheese, grated (about 1
    cup)
30  NABISCO TRISCUIT® Wafers
    Shredded lettuce
```

1. In large skillet, over medium-high heat, sauté beef and onion about 5 minutes, or until beef is no longer pink; drain fat. Stir in tomato sauce, water, chilies, chili powder, and salt. Bring to a boil; reduce heat to low; cover; simmer 20 minutes, stirring occasionally.
2. Preheat oven to 350° F. Grease 2-quart baking dish. In medium bowl, combine ricotta cheese and egg. Spoon ½ meat mixture into prepared dish; top with ½ Cheddar cheese and ½ ricotta cheese mixture. Arrange layer of 24 TRISCUIT Wafers over cheeses. Top with remaining ricotta cheese mixture, Cheddar cheese, and meat mixture. Coarsely break remaining 6 TRISCUIT Wafers; place over center of casserole. Bake, uncovered, 30 minutes, or until heated through.
3. To serve: Garnish with lettuce. Makes 6 servings.

SOUFFLÉ-TOPPED ITALIAN MEAT LOAF

This is a fantastic way to serve meat loaf. Thanks to the NABISCO kitchens for this unusual way of using WHEATS-WORTH® Stone Ground Wheat Crackers.

    32 WHEATSWORTH® Stone Ground
       Wheat Crackers
     1 egg
    ⅓ cup skim or regular milk
    ⅓ cup chopped onion
     1 teaspoon oregano
     1 pound lean ground beef

2 medium tomatoes, sliced

4 ounces part-skim mozzarella cheese,
grated (about ¾ cup)

3 eggs, separated, at room temperature

½ cup low-fat cottage cheese

Coarsely crush WHEATSWORTH Stone Ground Wheat Crackers to yield about 1¾ cups crumbs. Set aside 1½ cups crumbs for meat loaf, ¼ cup for soufflé topping.

In large bowl, using wire whisk, beat together 1 egg and milk; stir in 1½ cups WHEATSWORTH crumbs, onion, and oregano. Lightly mix in beef just to blend all ingredients. Spread evenly in 9-inch square baking dish; bake at 350° F for 20 minutes; remove from oven. Arrange tomato slices on top; sprinkle with mozzarella cheese; set aside.

In large bowl, with electric mixer at medium speed, beat together 3 egg yolks, cottage cheese, and ¼ cup WHEATSWORTH crumbs until fluffy, about 3 minutes; set aside.

In another large bowl, with electric mixer at high speed, beat egg whites until stiff but not dry. Fold, one-third at a time, into yolk mixture; spread on top of grated cheese. Bake 30 minutes. Serve immediately. Makes 6 servings.

To Microwave: Prepare WHEATSWORTH crumbs and meat loaf as directed above. Spread evenly in 8 × 8 × 2-inch microwave-proof baking dish; cook on high (100% power) for 9 to 10 minutes, rotating ½ turn every 3 minutes; remove from oven. Top with tomatoes and cheese.

Prepare soufflé topping as directed above. Microwave on high (100% power) 10 minutes, rotating ½ turn every 3 minutes, until top is no longer moist and looks firm. Serve immediately.

MOCK CABBAGE ROLLS

HEINZ Chili Sauce gives this easy recipe a great flavor.

    1 pound lean ground beef

    ½ cup chopped onion

    1 clove garlic, minced

    1 tablespoon shortening

    1 tablespoon paprika

    1 teaspoon salt

    ½ cup uncooked regular white rice

1½ cups water

    ¾ cup **HEINZ** Chili Sauce

    1 can (16 ounces) sauerkraut

Sauté beef, onion, and garlic in shortening until onion is tender; drain excess fat. Stir in paprika and salt, then rice, water, and chili sauce; heat to boiling. Evenly place half of the sauerkraut in bottom of baking dish (8 × 8 × 2 inches); carefully pour on hot meat mixture; top with remaining sauerkraut. Cover; bake in 350° F oven, 30 minutes. Remove cover; continue baking 15 to 20 minutes longer or until rice is tender. Serve topped with sour cream, if desired. Makes 6 servings.

SWEET-SOUR MEATBALLS

This is a basic recipe that can be used for party hors d'oeuvres or for family dinners.

1½ pounds lean ground beef

¾ cup dry bread crumbs

¼ cup milk

1 egg, slightly beaten

½ teaspoon salt

Dash pepper

1 can (8 to 8½ ounces) crushed pineapple

½ cup **HEINZ Apple Cider Vinegar**

¼ cup firmly packed brown sugar

2 tablespoons soy sauce

1 teaspoon ground ginger

1 tablespoon corn starch

1 tablespoon water

Combine first 6 ingredients, lightly but well. Form into 30 meatballs, using a rounded tablespoon for each. Drain pineapple; reserve liquid; cover pineapple; refrigerate. Add water to reserved liquid to measure ¾ cup. Combine this liquid with vinegar and next 3 ingredients in large skillet; heat to boiling; add meatballs. Cover; simmer 15 to 20 minutes or until meatballs are cooked; stir occasionally. Stir in drained pineapple. Combine corn starch and water; stir into meatballs; cook until sauce is thickened, stirring constantly. Makes 6 servings.

GREEK BURGERS

Hamburgers again! But this recipe will make hamburgers a joyous surprise.

4½ tablespoons **A.1. Steak Sauce**

1½ pounds ground beef

1 cup (4 ounces) Feta cheese, rinsed and crumbled

¼ cup sliced ripe olives

1 tablespoon **A.1. Steak Sauce**

1 teaspoon lemon juice

2 tablespoons mayonnaise

3 pita (or pocket) bread, cut in half

6 tomato slices

Shredded lettuce

Combine 4½ tablespoons A.1 and beef. Form 6 patties. Cook patties as desired. Combine cheese, olives, A.1., lemon juice, and mayonnaise. Place hamburgers in pita bread. Spoon topping over hamburgers. Heat in preheated 425° F oven 5 minutes. Garnish with tomato and lettuce. Serves 6.

MEATBALL SCALLOP

This is a hearty family meal that is easy to make on a busy day.

> 1 package <u>FRENCH'S Real Cheese Scalloped Potatoes</u>
>
> 1 pound lean ground beef
>
> ¼ cup dry bread crumbs
>
> 1 egg
>
> 2 tablespoons chopped green pepper
>
> 2 tablespoons mayonnaise
>
> ½ teaspoon onion salt

Mix ground beef, egg, bread crumbs, green pepper, mayonnaise, and onion salt. Shape mixture into 16 meatballs. Prepare potatoes as directed on the package, except use 2½ cups boiling water, ⅔ cup milk, 2 tablespoons butter (or margarine), and a 2-quart casserole. Bake potatoes in 400° F oven 15 minutes. Stir and top with meatballs, then bake 20 to 25 minutes longer. Serves 4 to 6.

POT ROAST GERMAN STYLE

A delicious dinner that gets a special flavor boost from HEINZ Garlic Wine Vinegar.

> 4 pounds rolled rump roast
>
> 1 tablespoon shortening

    1 teaspoon salt

  1/8 teaspoon pepper

1 1/2 cups water

  3/4 cup **HEINZ Garlic Wine Vinegar**

    1 medium onion, sliced

    2 bay leaves

  10 gingersnaps

In Dutch oven, brown meat on all sides in shortening. Season meat with salt and pepper. Add water, vinegar, onion, and bay leaves. Cover; simmer 2 1/2 hours or until meat is tender. Remove meat; discard bay leaves; skim excess fat from liquid. Add gingersnaps, several at a time, to liquid; stir to blend. Add meat; cover; simmer 10 to 15 minutes or until gravy is thickened. Makes 8 servings (about 3 1/2 cups gravy).

EASY BEEF STEW

When the weather outside is cold, warm up with this easy, satisfying stew.

    2 pounds beef for stew, cut in 1-inch
      cubes

    2 cups 1-inch pieces carrots

    2 cups 1-inch pieces celery

    2 cups quartered onions

    2 cups 1-inch pieces potatoes

    2 teaspoons salt

¼ teaspoon pepper

2 tablespoons MINUTE® Tapioca

¼ teaspoon each thyme and marjoram

1 bay leaf

2 cups tomato juice or beef broth

Combine all ingredients in 4-quart casserole. Cover and bake at 300° F for 2½ to 3 hours or at 250° F for 4½ to 5 hours, or until beef and vegetables are tender. Makes 9 cups or 8 servings.

RANCHERO SUPPER STEW

All-in-one skillet dinner that's sure to be a family pleaser. Use economical chuck beef to please the budget as well.

2 tablespoons oil

1½ pounds beef cubes

1 envelope LIPTON Onion or Beefy Onion Soup Mix

2 cans (16 ounces each) whole tomatoes, undrained

1 cup water

2 teaspoons chili powder

2 carrots, thinly sliced

1 green pepper, chopped

½ cup celery, thinly sliced

2 potatoes, diced

In large skillet, heat oil and brown beef; add LIPTON Onion Soup Mix blended with tomatoes, water, and chili powder. Simmer, stirring occasionally, 30 minutes. Add remaining ingredients. Simmer, covered, 45 minutes or until vegetables are tender and gravy is slightly thickened. Makes about 6 servings.

Microwave Directions: Omit water. In 3-quart casserole, heat beef 5 minutes, stirring once. Add remaining ingredients and heat, stirring occasionally, 10 minutes. Heat covered at medium (50% Full Power), stirring occasionally, 60 minutes or until beef is tender. Let stand covered 5 minutes.

OVEN-BAKED BOURGUIGNONNE

Keep in the freezer for unexpected company. Serve with hot buttered noodles and a fresh spinach salad.

- 2 pounds boneless chuck, cut into 1-inch cubes
- ¼ cup all-purpose flour
- 1⅓ cups sliced carrots
- 1 can (16 ounces) whole tomatoes, drained and chopped (reserve liquid)
- 1 envelope **LIPTON Beefy Onion or Onion Soup Mix**
- ½ cup dry red wine
- 1 bay leaf
- 1 cup sliced mushrooms

Preheat oven to 400° F. In 2-quart casserole, toss beef with flour and bake uncovered 20 minutes. Add carrots, tomatoes, and LIPTON Beefy Onion Soup Mix blended with reserved liquid, wine, and bay leaf. Bake covered 1½ hours or until beef is tender. Add mushrooms and bake covered an additional 10 minutes. Makes about 8 servings.

Freezing/Reheating Directions: Tightly wrap covered casserole in heavy-duty foil; freeze. To reheat, unwrap and bake covered at 400° F, stirring occasionally to separate beef and vegetables, 1 hour. *OR,* microwave, stirring occasionally, 20 minutes or until heated through. Let stand covered 5 minutes.

Microwave Directions: Toss beef with flour; set aside. In 2-quart casserole, combine tomatoes and LIPTON Beefy Onion Soup Mix blended with reserved liquid, wine, and bay leaf. Heat covered 7 minutes, stirring once. Add beef and carrots. Heat covered at Defrost (30% Full Power), stirring occasionally, 1¼ hours. Add mushrooms and heat covered at Defrost, 30 minutes or until beef is tender. Let stand covered 5 minutes.

SPAGHETTI BRAVISSIMO

The easiest spaghetti you've ever made! Serve with salad and garlic bread for a quick meal.

    1 envelope **LIPTON Onion Soup Mix**
    1 package (8 ounces) spaghetti
 1½ quarts boiling water
    1 pound ground beef
    1 can (8 ounces) tomato sauce

1 can (7 ounces) tomato paste

1 tablespoon parsley flakes

1 teaspoon oregano

½ teaspoon sweet basil

In large saucepan, combine LIPTON Onion Soup Mix and spaghetti with water; cook 20 minutes or until spaghetti is tender. Do not drain. In large skillet, brown meat; stir in tomato sauce and paste, parsley, oregano, and basil. Add to onion soup and spaghetti in the saucepan and heat through. Makes about 4 servings.

HEARTY MANICOTTI

This nutritious cheese filled Italian dish is ideal for both family and friends.

Water

1 pound Italian sweet sausage links

1 pound ground beef

1 medium onion chopped

2 8-ounce cans tomato puree

1 6-ounce can tomato paste

1 teaspoon sugar

½ teaspoon pepper

Basil

Salt

1 8-ouncepackage Manicotti shells

1 15-ounce container **SARGENTO** Ricotta Cheese

2 cups **SARGENTO** Shredded Mozzarella
Cheese

2 tablespoons chopped parsley

SARGENTO Grated Italian Style Cheese

Combine ¼ cup water and sausage in a 5-quart covered Dutch oven, cook for 5 minutes over medium heat. Uncover, allow sausage to brown well, remove and drain on paper towels.

Remove fat from Dutch oven: over medium heat brown ground beef and onion. Stir in tomato puree, tomato paste, sugar, pepper, 1 teaspoon basil, 1 teaspoon salt and 1 cup water; cover and simmer 45 minutes.

Cut drained sausage into bite-size pieces; add to tomato and ground beef mixture; simmer another 15 minutes, stirring occasionally. Meanwhile, cook manicotti as label directs; rinse and drain well. Preheat oven to 375° F.

In a large bowl, combine Ricotta and Mozzarella cheeses, parsley, ¾ teaspoon basil and ½ teaspoon salt. Stuff cheese mixture into shells and set aside.

Spoon one half of meat sauce into a 13 × 9-inch baking pan. Arrange half of the cheese stuffed shells in the pan. Spoon meat sauce over shells, retaining ¾ cup. Arrange remaining shells in pan and cover with reserved meat sauce. Sprinkle with Italian Style Grated Cheese. Bake 30 minutes. Makes 8 servings.

TACO PIZZA

A made-from-scratch pizza that's worth the effort. The crisp, tender crust is an interesting variation on traditional pizza crust.

Crust

6 tablespoons butter or margarine, softened

1 egg

1 cup plus 2 tablespoons flour*

2 cups **CORN CHEX Cereal** crushed to ½ cup

½ teaspoon salt

¼ cup water

Filling

½ pound ground beef

1 teaspoon chili powder

½ teaspoon salt

¼ teaspoon ground cumin

1 can (8.5 ounces) refried beans

1 can (4 ounces) chopped green chilies (do not drain)

2 medium tomatoes, chopped, salted

½ cup chopped onion

¼ cup coarsely chopped green pepper

½ cup (2 ounces) shredded Monterey Jack cheese

½ cup (2 ounces) shredded Cheddar
cheese
Taco sauce

Preheat oven to 450° F. To make *Crust:* butter 12-inch pizza pan. In small bowl of electric mixer, cream butter. Add egg. (Mixture will separate.) Slowly mix in flour, CHEX brand cereal crumbs, and salt until crumbs form. Pour in water. Mix until thoroughly blended. Form into ball (dough may be slightly wet). With fingers, press into pan up to edge. Bake 8 to 10 minutes or until edges begin to brown.

For *Filling:* cook and stir ground beef, chili powder, salt, and cumin in medium skillet until browned. Add beans, chilies, and chilies' liquid. Spread evenly over crust.

Arrange tomatoes in ring around edge of crust. Place onions in ring inside tomatoes. Put green peppers in center. Sprinkle with cheeses. Bake 10 to 12 minutes or until hot and cheese is melted. Serve with taco sauce. Makes 8 servings.

*Stir flour; then spoon into measuring cup.

REUBEN STRATA

This easy dish will satisfy hungry appetites. Make it in larger quantities and it is terrific for a party.

36 **WHEATSWORTH®** Stone Ground
   Wheat Crackers
 6 ounces Swiss cheese, grated (about 1½
   cups)

1 (8-ounce) can sauerkraut, well drained

8 ounces corned beef, diced

1 tablespoon chopped parsley

3 eggs

1½ cups milk

⅓ cup bottled Russian dressing

In lightly greased 1½-quart shallow baking dish, arrange 3 rows of 4 WHEATSWORTH Stone Ground Wheat Crackers. Set aside ⅓ cup cheese. Layer half of remaining cheese, half of sauerkraut, and half of corned beef; repeat layers. Top with a third layer of crackers. Blend reserved cheese with parsley; sprinkle over top. Beat together eggs, milk, and dressing; pour evenly over casserole. Bake at 350° F for 35 to 40 minutes, or until puffed and golden brown. Makes 4 servings.

Note: Recipe may be assembled a day in advance and refrigerated. Bake an additional 10 minutes.

BLANQUETTE

This recipe cooks with a flair, and tastes equally good using veal or lamb.

3 pounds cubed, boneless veal or lamb

3 cups boiling water

3 teaspoons **HERB-OX** Instant Chicken Style Bouillon or 3 **HERB-OX** Chicken Bouillon Cubes

6 carrots

 1 teaspoon lemon juice

 1 can (1 pound) small white onions

 1 can (8 ounces) mushroom caps
  (optional)

 3 tablespoons butter

 3 tablespoons flour

 2 egg yolks

½ cup cream or milk

Cover cubed meat with boiling water, add instant bouillon or bouillon cubes, stir. Simmer, covered, about 1 hour. Add carrots, cook until meat is tender. Remove meat and carrots to a serving dish. Boil pan liquid rapidly to reduce it to 1½ cups. Melt butter in a small pan, stir in flour, add reduced liquid and cook, stirring, until sauce is smooth and thickened. Beat egg yolks with milk, warm with a little sauce, combine. Add more instant bouillon to taste. Add lemon juice. Add meat, carrots, onions, and mushrooms, reheat without boiling. Makes 8 servings.

APPLE HARVEST PORK CHOPS

Here is a new, easy way to serve pork chops.

6 loin pork chops, cut ½- to ¾-inch thick
1 tablespoon shortening
   Salt and pepper
1 jar (15 ounces) apple sauce
½ cup **HEINZ Chili Sauce**
3 tablespoons minced onion
2 tablespoons minced parsley (optional)
1 teaspoon **HEINZ Apple Cider Vinegar**
¾ teaspoon salt
   Dash pepper

Brown chops well in shortening; drain excess fat. Season chops lightly with salt and pepper. Combine apple sauce and remaining ingredients; pour over chops. Cover; simmer 1 hour, basting occasionally, or until chops are tender. Makes 6 servings (about 2 cups sauce).

BEANS AND HAM ALOHA

Serve with bread and a salad, and you'll enjoy a great meal.

  1 28-ounce can **B&M Brick Oven Baked Beans**
  1 1½-pound fully cooked ham steak, cut into bite-size pieces
  2 pineapple rings, cut in halves
  2 tablespoons brown sugar

In a large bowl, combine beans and ham. Pour into a 2-quart casserole. Top with pineapple slices and sprinkle with brown sugar. Bake at 350° F for 30 minutes. Makes 6 servings.

SPEEDY BAKED BEANS WITH WIENERS

A family favorite that's fast and can be doubled to feed a crowd.

  10 slices OSCAR MAYER® Bacon
   3 cans (1 pound each) baked beans in molasses sauce

1 medium onion, chopped

¼ cup firmly packed brown sugar

1 tablespoon molasses

2 teaspoons Worcestershire sauce

½ teaspoon dry mustard

1 package (16 ounces) **OSCAR MAYER®**
   Cheese Hot Dogs

Cut bacon into 1-inch pieces; cook in skillet until crisp. Add onion to bacon; cook until tender. Stir in remaining ingredients. Place wieners on top of beans. Heat 15 minutes more. Serves 6.

Microwave: Cut bacon into 1-inch pieces. Place in 2-quart glass casserole; cover with paper towel. Microwave 7 to 9 minutes or until crisp, stirring twice with 2 forks to separate pieces. Add onion; cover with paper towel. Microwave at HIGH 2 minutes or until tender. Add remaining ingredients; cover. Microwave at HIGH 8 minutes, stirring halfway through heating.

CAMPER'S WIENER STEW

No mixing or measuring . . . just combine and heat over a campfire or a cookstove.

1 package (16 ounces) **OSCAR MAYER®**
   Wieners

1 can (10¾ ounces) vegetable soup

1 can (16 ounces) whole white potatoes,
   drained and quartered

   1 can (16 ounces) sliced carrots, drained

   1 can (5½ ounces) tomato juice

  ¼ teaspoon thyme

Cut wieners into 1-inch pieces. Combine with remaining ingredients in saucepan. Bring to a boil. Cover. Turn down heat. Simmer 10 minutes. Makes 4 servings.

CHILI BEANS

This is an inexpensive, hearty dish, great for indoor or outdoor meals, year round.

   1 tablespoon butter or margarine

   1 tablespoon chopped onion

   1 teaspoon chili powder

  ½ pound frankfurts, cut into 1-inch pieces

   1 28-ounce can **B&M Brick Oven Baked Beans**

In a skillet, melt butter or margarine, and add onions, chili powder, and frankfurts. Sauté frankfurts until lightly browned. In a 2-quart casserole, combine frankfurts and beans; bake at 350° F for 30 minutes. Makes 4 servings.

CHOUCROUTE GARNI

A feast in a skillet, this hearty, German-influenced dish from Alsace, France is just right for cool autumn and winter days.

  4 slices OSCAR MAYER® Bacon

  2 jars (32 ounces each) CLAUSSEN® Sauerkraut, drained

  4 medium carrots, thinly sliced

  3 medium onions, chopped

  1 can (10¾ ounces) chicken broth

  ¾ cup dry white wine

  12 whole black peppercorns

  10 juniper berries (optional)

  1 package (16 ounces) OSCAR MAYER® Wieners

  1 package (12 ounces) OSCAR MAYER® Ring Bologna

  1 package (8 ounces) OSCAR MAYER® Ham Steaks

  1 package (5 ounces) OSCAR MAYER® "Little Smokies"

Cut bacon into 1-inch pieces. Cook in Dutch oven or large saucepot on medium-low until crisp. Add remaining ingredients except meat. Bring to a boil. Turn down heat. Cover. Simmer 15 minutes. Add meat. Cover. Simmer 15 minutes more. Serves 8.

HAM ROLL-UPS WITH MORNAY SAUCE

SARA LEE All-Butter Croissants makes this recipe extra special and easy.

8 slices baked ham

8 slices Swiss cheese

8 asparagus spears, cooked

8 frozen **SARA LEE All-Butter Croissants**

Mornay Sauce (see recipe)

Place 2 ham slices overlapping slightly on flat surface. Place 2 cheese slices over ham. Top with 2 asparagus spears; roll up. Repeat process. Arrange roll-ups in lightly buttered baking dish. Heat in preheated 325° F oven 12 minutes. Cut frozen croissants in half lengthwise; leave together. Heat frozen croissants on ungreased baking sheet in preheated 325° F oven 9 to 11 minutes. Place 1 ham roll-up on each croissant bottom half. Spoon on Mornay Sauce. Top with remaining croissant half. Makes 4 servings.

MORNAY SAUCE

2 tablespoons butter

2 tablespoons flour

1 cup milk

½ cup shredded Swiss cheese

⅛ teaspoon ground nutmeg

Heat butter in small saucepan. Add flour; cook until bubbly. Gradually stir in milk. Cook until thickened. Stir in cheese until smooth. Stir in nutmeg. Makes 4 servings.

SPECIALTY OF THE HOUSE SANDWICH

A great sandwich from **OSCAR MAYER** . . . certain to become the favorite at your house as well!

2 slices OSCAR MAYER® Bacon

1 large slice rye bread, toasted

1 leaf lettuce

2 slices OSCAR MAYER® Braunschweiger

2 slices tomato

4 slices avocado

2 tablespoons Thousand Island dressing

Cook bacon according to package directions; drain. Place toasted bread on dinner plate. Top with lettuce leaf and braunschweiger. Arrange tomato and avocado over braunschweiger. Top with bacon. Spoon dressing over top. Makes 1 sandwich.

TWICE FRIED PORK WITH GINGER SAUCE

In Oriental cooking, batter-fried foods such as pork are often cooked twice for extra crispness. Corn starch in the batter also contributes to the crispness.

> 1 pound boneless pork
>
> 1 tablespoon soy sauce
>
> 1 tablespoon dry sherry
>
> 1/4 teaspoon ground cinnamon
>
> 1/4 teaspoon pepper
>
> 1/8 teaspoon ground cloves
>
> 1/2 cup flour
>
> 1/3 cup **ARGO®** or **KINGSFORD'S®** Corn Starch
>
> 3/4 cup water
>
> 1 tablespoon corn oil
>
> 1 egg white
>
> 1 quart (about) corn oil
>
> Ginger Sauce (recipe follows)

Cut pork into 1/2-inch slices, then into 1-inch squares. In medium bowl stir together soy sauce, sherry, cinnamon, pepper, and cloves. Add pork; toss well. Cover; refrigerate while preparing batter. In large bowl stir together flour and corn starch. Gradually stir in water until smooth. Stir in 1 tablespoon corn oil. Let stand 30 minutes. Beat egg white until stiff peaks form; fold into batter. Pour corn oil into heavy 3-quart saucepan or deep fryer, filling no more than 1/3 full. Heat over medium-high heat to 375° F. Dip pork into batter and fry, a few pieces at a time, 3 to 4 minutes or until golden. Drain on paper towels. Prepare Ginger Sauce. Before serving, reheat corn oil over medium-high heat to 375° F. Fry pork, a few pieces at a time, about 1 minute or until batter is very crisp. Drain on paper towels. Serve immediately with Ginger Sauce. Makes 4 to 6 servings.

GINGER SAUCE

Oriental cooking uses corn starch for thickening sauces because it produces a translucent appearance and lets the flavor of the foods come through.

  1 tablespoon **ARGO®** or **KINGSFORD'S®** Corn Starch*

¾ cup water

  3 tablespoons catsup

  2 tablespoons soy sauce

  2 tablespoons dry sherry

  2 tablespoons corn oil

¼ pound snow peas

½ cup sliced water chestnuts

  1 red small sweet pepper, diced

  1 medium onion, cut into 8 wedges, layers separated

  1 clove garlic, minced or pressed

  2 teaspoons finely grated fresh ginger, or ½ teaspoon ground ginger

In small bowl stir together corn starch, water, catsup, soy sauce, and sherry until smooth. In large skillet heat corn oil over medium heat. Add snow peas, water chestnuts, pepper, onion, garlic, and ginger. Stir fry 2 to 3 minutes or until vegetables are tender crisp. Restir corn starch mixture; add to vegetables. Stirring constantly, bring to boil over medium heat and boil 1 minute. Serve over Twice Fried Pork. Makes about 2 cups.

*This recipe was sent to us by the makers of ARGO® and KINGSFORD'S® Corn Starch. ARGO, KINGSFORD'S are registered trademarks of CPC International Inc.

NACHO ENCHILADAS

Easy enchiladas made with *new* nacho-style cheese hot dogs from **OSCAR MAYER.**

   2 cans (10 ounces each) enchilada sauce

 10 flour tortillas, 6-inch diameter

   1 package (16 ounces) **OSCAR MAYER®**
      Nacho-Style Cheese Hot Dogs

   1 medium onion, finely chopped

 ½ cup sour cream

      Sliced ripe olives

   1 green onion with top, chopped

Pour 1 can enchilada sauce in 13 × 9-inch pan. Roll a tortilla around each hot dog. Place seam side down in pan. Sprinkle with onion. Top with remaining can enchilada sauce. Bake in 350° F oven 30 minutes. Garnish with sour cream, olives, and green onion. Makes 5 servings.

QUICHE LORRAINE

Serve Quiche Lorraine any time of day. This versatile dish is at home for breakfast, brunch, lunch, or dinner. Experiment with your favorite substitutions—ham for bacon as an example—and create your own unique recipe.

8 slices cooked bacon

9 -inch unbaked pie shell

1½ cups (6 ounces) shredded Swiss cheese

½ cup thinly sliced onion rings

1 tablespoon flour

½ teaspoon salt

¼ teaspoon pepper

1½ cups *undiluted* **CARNATION Evaporated Milk**

3 beaten eggs

Crumble bacon in unbaked pie shell. Cover with cheese and onion. Combine flour, salt, and pepper. Gradually stir in evaporated milk. Add beaten eggs to evaporated milk mixture; blend well. Pour over cheese and onions. Bake in moderate oven (375° F) 30 to 40 minutes, or until knife inserted halfway between center and edge comes out clean. Let stand 5 minutes before serving. Makes one 9-inch pie.

BARBECUED SPARERIBS

This is a super recipe you'll enjoy over and over again.

2 pounds pork spareribs

1 cup apple juice

1 tablespoon soy sauce

2 tablespoons hoisin sauce or catsup

1 tablespoon honey

1 packet SWEET 'N LOW

In large saucepan of boiling water, simmer ribs about 5 minutes to remove excess fat. Drain. In shallow baking dish, combine remaining ingredients. Add ribs and marinate 2 to 3 hours. Preheat oven to 350° F. Bake, uncovered, 45 minutes. Increase temperature to 450° F and continue baking 5 to 10 minutes, or until very tender. About 24 ribs.

MEXICAN MELT

A great idea for singles or a crowd. Serve for breakfast, lunch, or as a snack, just 215 calories each.

1 square (3 ounces) frozen shredded hash brown potatoes

½ tablespoon vegetable oil

1 slice LOUIS RICH™ Turkey Ham

½ slice process American cheese, cut
diagonally

1 tablespoon chopped green chilies

Taco sauce (optional)

Brown potatoes in oil in small skillet according to package directions. Top with turkey ham, cheese, and chilies. Turn off heat. Cover. Let stand for about 1 minute to melt cheese. Serve with taco sauce. Serves 1.

BOLOGNA RELLENOS

A taste of Mexico with a healthy twist. Turkey bologna is lower in fat and lower in calories than regular bologna. Try this favorite recipe for your next party.

3 packages (8 ounces each) **LOUIS RICH**℠ **Turkey Bologna**

1 package (16 ounces) flour tortillas,
8-inch diameter

1 package (8 ounces) Monterey Jack
cheese, cut into 12 (½-inch) strips

12 mild banana peppers

½ cup (4 ounces) taco sauce

Oil for frying or ¼ cup melted butter for
baking

Toothpicks

Frying Method: For each serving, place 2 slices meat on a tortilla. Top with 1 strip cheese and 1 pepper; roll up and secure with toothpicks. Heat oil (about 1 inch deep) in heavy skillet or deep-fat fryer to 350° F. Fry in hot oil 2 to 3 minutes, turning to brown evenly on all sides. Drain on paper toweling. Heat taco sauce. Serve over Bologna Rellenos. Makes 12 servings.

Baking Method: For each serving, place 2 slices bologna on each tortilla. Top with 1 strip cheese and 1 pepper; fold opposite edges over filling and tuck ends under. Place meat packets seam side down on ungreased baking sheet; brush generously with butter. Bake in 400° F oven 15 to 20 minutes until crisp and golden brown. Heat taco sauce. Serve over Bologna Rellenos. Makes 12 servings.

POULTRY DISHES

CHICKEN ACAPULCO

Don't be afraid to try Chicken Acapulco. It's one Mexican-style dish that won't overwhelm you with hot seasoning. The delicate egg mixture covers the chicken, cheeses, and chilies and bakes to a puffy, golden brown like a relleno. Top with just the right amount of salsa to satisfy your taste buds.

    2 tablespoons butter
    6 (about 1½ pounds) boned, skinned,
       chicken breast halves

¾ cup (3 ounces) shredded Cheddar
   cheese
¾ cup (3 ounces) shredded Jack cheese
½ cup (4-ounce can) diced green chilies
½ cup finely chopped onion
1 cup *undiluted* **CARNATION Evaporated
   Milk**
¼ cup flour
4 egg yolks
⅓ cup water
½ teaspoon salt
4 egg whites
1 cup (7- or 8-ounce can) green chili salsa

Melt butter in $12 \times 7\frac{1}{2} \times 2$-inch baking dish. Place chicken in dish. Bake in moderate oven (350° F) 30 minutes. Drain off fat. Combine cheeses, chilies, and onion in medium bowl. Sprinkle over chicken breasts. Stir small amount of evaporated milk into flour to make a paste. Gradually stir in remaining evaporated milk. Add egg yolks, water, and salt; mix well. Beat egg whites until stiff but not dry. Fold into milk mixture. Carefully pour over chicken and cheese mixture. Bake 20 to 25 minutes or until puffed and lightly browned. Heat chili salsa to serving temperature. Serve with chicken. Makes $12 \times 7\frac{1}{2} \times 2$-inch casserole.

BAKED YOGURT CHICKEN

Healthful and delicious. Enjoy it often.

1 cut-up frying chicken, 2½ to 3 pounds
  Salt, pepper
6 tablespoons butter or margarine
2 tablespoons flour
1 tablespoon paprika
2 cups **DANNON** **Plain Yogurt**
¼ pound fresh mushrooms, cleaned and
  sliced
2 tablespoons fresh lemon juice
2 tablespoons chopped fresh dill or
  parsley

Wash chicken pieces and wipe dry. Add salt and pepper. In a large pan, melt 4 tablespoons of butter, fry chicken until golden brown. Remove to buttered shallow baking dish. Sprinkle flour and paprika into pan juices and cook, stirring, for 2 minutes. Stir in yogurt and mix well. Spoon over chicken. Sauté mushrooms in remaining 2 tablespoons of butter and lemon juice for 1 minute and spoon over pan. Sprinkle with the dill. Bake, covered, in preheated moderate oven (325° F) for about 1 to 1¼ hours, or until chicken is tender. Serves about 4.

CRISPY COCONUT CHICKEN

The coconut makes this chicken dish special enough for company, yet it's so simple to prepare that you will serve it to your family often.

1⅓ cups **BAKER'S® ANGEL FLAKE®** <u>Coconut</u>

½ cup seasoned bread crumbs

3 pounds frying chicken pieces

1 egg, well beaten

2 tablespoons water

⅓ cup melted butter or margarine

Mix coconut with bread crumbs. Mix egg with water. Dip chicken pieces in egg; coat with coconut mixture. Place in shallow baking pan; drizzle with melted butter. Bake at 400° F for about 1 hour, or until chicken is tender. Baste once with pan drippings. Makes 6 servings.

CHICKEN CHUT-NUT CREPES

This is a sophisticated, excellent recipe that is made special with G. B. RAFFETTO® Chut-Nut. RAFFETTO has a whole line of products that make it easy to produce similar stunning results.

1 small onion, chopped

⅓ cup chopped celery

4 tablespoons butter or margarine

3 tablespoons flour

¼ teaspoon salt

⅛ teaspoon pepper

2 packages MBT Chicken Broth

1 cup water

¾ cup heavy cream

¼ cup **RAFFETTO** Chut-Nut

½ teaspoon lemon juice

3 cups diced cooked chicken

12 7-inch crepes (see recipe)

In large saucepan, sauté onion and celery in butter until tender. Blend in flour, salt, and pepper until smooth. Stir in chicken broth and water; cook over medium heat, stirring constantly, until mixture thickens and boils. Add cream; heat just to boiling, stirring constantly. Remove ½ cup sauce and reserve. Stir Chut-Nut and lemon juice into saucepan; add chicken. Spoon about ¼ cup chicken mixture in center of each crepe; roll up. Place crepes, seam side down, in lightly greased baking dish, about 12 × 8 inches. Spoon reserved sauce down center of crepes. Bake in 425° F oven about 10 minutes or until hot.

To make crepes: combine 2 eggs, 1½ cups flour, 2 cups milk, ½ teaspoon salt, and 2 tablespoons salad oil in electric blender; whirl until smooth. Cover and refrigerate at least 1 hour. To bake crepes, heat a 7-inch crepe pan or skillet until hot; add a little butter to grease lightly. Pour in about ¼ cup batter; tilt and turn pan to spread batter over bottom. Cook until lightly browned on bottom; turn and cook 1 minute longer. To store crepes, stack with a piece of wax paper between each crepe. Makes 6 servings.

HONG KONG CHICKEN

A very popular Chinese dish.

>   2 pounds boneless and skinless chicken
>   1 onion, sliced thin
>   1 cup celery, sliced thin on diagonal
>   1 green bell pepper, cut in strips
>   1 can sliced water chestnuts, drained
>   1 can sliced bamboo shoots, drained
>   1 16-ounce can bean sprouts, rinsed and drained
> 1/2 pound Chinese snow pea pods, fresh or frozen and thawed
>   1 cup chicken broth or bouillon
>   1 teaspoon MSG (optional)
>   1 teaspoon salt or to taste
> 1/4 teaspoon ground ginger
> 2–3 tablespoons soy sauce
>   1 bottle **WALDEN FARMS Reduced Calorie Creamy French Dressing**

Marinate chicken in dressing. Combine chicken, green pepper, celery, onion, water chestnuts, bamboo shoots, broth, MSG, salt, and ginger in electric skillet set at

350° F. Cook covered for 7 minutes. Add soy sauce, bean sprouts, and snow peas. Reduce heat to 250° F and simmer uncovered for 3 minutes. Stir occasionally, adding more broth if too dry. Serves 4 to 6.

MANDARIN CHICKEN

Economical, easy recipe that is perfect for family meals or parties.

  2 broiler-fryer chickens cut in serving
    pieces
½ cup soy sauce
¼ cup orange juice
  1 cup **MINUTE MAID**® Lemon Juice
  1 cup corn oil
  1 cup chopped onion
  1 tablespoon curry powder
  1 tablespoon chili powder
  2 teaspoons MSG (monosodium
    glutamate)

Mix together soy sauce, orange juice, MINUTE MAID Lemon Juice, corn oil, onion, curry powder, chili powder, and MSG. Place chicken in shallow dish and pour on marinade. Cover with aluminum foil. Marinate in refrigerator at least 2 hours, turning occasionally. Line large shallow pan or broiler pan with aluminum foil. Drain chicken pieces, reserving marinade. Place chicken on prepared pan. Broil or grill chicken about 6 inches from source of heat, basting with reserved marinade, 15 minutes on each side, or until tender and brown. Yield: 8 servings.

FAMILY STIR-FRY

This easy, skillet dinner is so good, it will become one of your prized recipes.

　1　can (20 ounces) <u>DOLE Chunk Pineapple in Juice or Syrup</u>
　2　whole chicken breasts, split, boned
　2　tablespoons soy sauce
　4　stalks green onion
　1　large carrot
　2　cloves garlic, pressed
　1　tablespoon minced ginger root
　3　tablespoons sesame oil
　½　cup toasted peanuts
　4　cups shredded lettuce

Drain pineapple. Cut chicken into bite-size chunks. Toss chicken with soy sauce. Chop white part of green onion. Cut green part in 1-inch pieces. Slice carrot in thin slivers. Add chopped onion, garlic, ginger root, and sesame oil to wok or skillet. Add chicken and stir-fry until it just turns white. Remove from skillet with slotted spoon. Stir in carrots and peanuts. Cook 1 minute. Add pineapple, heat through. Return chicken to skillet. Stir in lettuce, green part of onion and stir-fry about 30 seconds. Serve with rice. Makes 4 servings.

SAVORY PRUNE CHICKEN

If you've never tasted chicken prepared with prunes, you owe it to yourself to try this great recipe. Once you do, you'll use it again and again.

3½ pounds frying chicken, cut-up pieces

1½ teaspoons salt

2 tablespoons oil

1 small onion, chopped

1 carrot, pared and sliced

1 cup **SUNSWEET** Pitted Prunes

1 cup water

1½ tablespoons corn starch

2 tablespoons cold water

Sprinkle chicken pieces with 1 teaspoon of the salt. In a heavy skillet, brown chicken in heated oil; remove chicken. Add onion and cook until soft. Add carrots and prunes; return chicken to skillet. Add the 1 cup water and remaining ½ teaspoon salt. Bring to a boil; cover, reduce heat, and simmer 30 minutes or until chicken is tender. Remove chicken to serving dish. Skim off and discard any fat from pan liquid. Mix corn starch with the 2 tablespoons cold water. Blend into carrot-prune mixture and cook, stirring, until thickened. Pour over chicken. Makes 4 to 6 servings.

CHICKEN AND RICE SEVILLE

This splendid blend of ingredients will satisfy hungry appetites.

1 large (about 3 pounds) cut-up frying chicken
2 tablespoons flour
1 teaspoon salt
⅛ teaspoon pepper
⅔ cup (6-ounce can) CONTADINA Tomato Paste
1¼ cups (10¾-ounce can) condensed chicken broth
1 cup chopped onion
1 cup raw rice
1 bay leaf
1 teaspoon oregano leaves
1½ teaspoons chili powder
½ teaspoon garlic salt
1 cup water
1⅔ cups (14½-ounce can) **CONTADINA** Stewed Tomatoes

Place chicken pieces in small paper or plastic bag filled with flour, salt, and pepper mixture. Shake bag to coat chicken well. Place chicken in 13 × 9 × 2-inch baking dish. Bake in hot oven (400° F) 30 minutes. Drain off fat. Combine tomato paste with remaining ingredients. Pour over chicken, lifting chicken pieces to top of rice mixture. Cover with aluminum foil. Reduce heat to 350° F and bake 1 hour. Makes 4 to 6 servings.

ITALIAN BONELESS CHICKEN

Enjoy half of this delicious cheesy entree now, freeze the other half and bake later.

  6 beaten eggs

  2 cups **SARGENTO** Grated Parmesan & Romano cheeses (8 ounces)

  ½ cup fine dry bread crumbs

  4 cups finely chopped cooked chicken

  3 tablespoons butter

  ½ cup chopped green pepper

  ½ cup chopped onion

  1 tablespoon cooking oil

  2 15-ounce cans tomato sauce

  1 teaspoon sugar

  ½ teaspoon Italian seasoning

  ¼ teaspoon dried basil, crushed

  ¼ teaspoon garlic powder

  ⅛ teaspoon pepper

  2 cups **SARGENTO** Shredded Mozzarella Cheese (8 ounces)

Combine eggs, SARGENTO Grated Parmesan & Romano cheese, and crumbs. Stir in chicken; mix well. With hands, shape mixture into sixteen ¾-inch-thick patties. In a large skillet cook patties in butter over medium-high heat for 2 to 3 minutes per side or till browned. Drain patties; arrange in two 10×6×2-inch baking dishes. Cook green pepper and onion in hot oil till tender. Remove from heat. Add ½ cup water and remaining ingredients except Mozzarella. Spoon sauce over patties; sprinkle with SARGENTO Shredded Mozzarella. Bake one casserole, uncovered, in 350° F oven for 25 minutes or till hot. Wrap, label, and freeze remaining casserole. (Bake frozen casserole, covered, in 400° F oven, for 50 minutes; uncover and bake 20 minutes more or till heated through.) Makes 2 casseroles, 4 or 5 servings each.

WALDEN ITALIAN CORNISH HENS WITH VEGETABLES

It's great! Use this to make your dinner party really special.

⅔ cup **WALDEN FARMS Reduced Calorie Italian Dressing**

¼ cup dry white wine

2 Cornish hens, split in half

1½ teaspoons garlic powder

2 small fresh zucchini, sliced

2 small fresh ripe tomatoes, cut in quarters

1 medium onion, sliced

Combine WALDEN FARMS Dressing and wine. Set aside. Rub hens with garlic powder. Place hens on a rack in

a shallow pan. Roast hens in 375° F oven, basting occasionally with salad dressing mixture, for 40 minutes.
Place zucchini, tomatoes, and onion in bottom of pan
and continue to bake and baste for 20 minutes more
or until zucchini is tender. Serve hens with the vegetables. Serves 4.

TURKEY PARMIGIANA

Use turkey breast slices just like veal! The light, delicate
flavor of turkey enhances the most subtle sauces.

1 package (1 pound) **LOUIS RICH**℠
Turkey Breast slices

1 egg, slightly beaten

2 tablespoons salad oil

1/3 cup seasoned dry bread crumbs

3 ounces tomato paste

3/4 cup chicken broth

1 clove garlic, finely chopped

1 teaspoon oregano leaves

4 ounces Mozzarella cheese

Chopped parsley

Dip turkey into mixture of egg blended with oil; coat
lightly with bread crumbs. Arrange turkey in a single
layer on a cookie sheet. Bake in 450° F oven 8 to 10
minutes until lightly browned. Meanwhile, combine tomato paste, broth, garlic, and oregano in small saucepan. Simmer over medium heat until thickened, about
10 minutes. Arrange turkey on an oven-proof platter.
Spoon tomato mixture over turkey. Top with cheese;

broil 2 minutes or until cheese bubbles. Garnish with parsley. Serves 4.

TURKEY A L'ORANGE

Elegant and easy . . . these fresh turkey tenderloins are ready in just 20 minutes.

> 1 package (1 to 2 pounds) **LOUIS RICH**℠ **Fresh Turkey Tenderloins**
>
> 1 tablespoon firmly packed brown sugar
>
> 2 teaspoons corn starch
>
> ½ cup orange juice
>
> 1½ teaspoons lemon juice
>
> 1 teaspoon butter
>
> Fresh orange slices
>
> 1 tablespoon brandy (optional)

Place turkey on broiler pan. Broil 5 inches from heat 10 minutes; turn. Broil 10 minutes more. Meanwhile, prepare sauce by combining sugar and corn starch in saucepan. Add juices and butter; cook, stirring constantly, on medium heat until sauce thickens and boils. Pour sauce over turkey and garnish with orange slices to serve. Serves 2.

To flame (optional): Heat brandy in small pan over low heat until it begins to sizzle along the sides of pan when tilted. Remove from heat. Using a long match, light brandy; pour over turkey and sauce. If flaming is not desired, the brandy can be stirred in after the sauce is thickened.

MONTE CRISTO SANDWICH

The Count never had it so good! Sprinkle your Monte Cristo sandwich with powdered sugar or serve with raspberry jam.

    1 slice **LOUIS RICH**™ **Turkey Ham**

    1 slice Swiss cheese

    1 slice **LOUIS RICH**™ **Oven-Roasted**

        Turkey Breast

    2 slices frozen French toast

Layer turkey ham, cheese, and oven-roasted turkey between French toast. Place on ungreased baking sheet and heat in a 400° F oven for 15 minutes. Makes 1 sandwich.

MEATLESS MAIN DISHES

Bagels are American favorites, popular for breakfast through midnight snacks. Use them for main meals with interesting toppings.

PIZZA BAGEL

Spread both halves of a **LENDER'S**® Bagel with tomato sauce. Top each half with Mozzarella cheese. Broil until cheese is bubbly. (For variety, add your choice of strips of cooked bacon, mushrooms, anchovies, or peppers.)

TUNA ITALIANO

Spread both halves of a **LENDER'S**® Bagel with tuna-fish salad spiced with oregano. Top each half with a tomato slice and a slice of Muenster cheese. Broil until cheese melts.

CHEESE PUFF

You'll be so pleased with this easy and imaginative Cheese Puff that you will want to use it frequently.

- 35 **RITZ**® Crackers, coarsely broken
- 8 ounces sharp Cheddar cheese, grated (about 2 cups)
- 1 (4-ounce) can sliced mushrooms, drained
- 4 eggs, slightly beaten
- 2½ cups milk
- 1 tablespoon instant minced onion
- 1 tablespoon parsley flakes
- ¼ teaspoon poultry seasoning

In greased 1-quart soufflé dish, layer RITZ Crackers, Cheddar cheese, and mushrooms. In medium bowl, with electric mixer at medium speed, beat together eggs, milk, onion, parsley, and poultry seasoning until well blended. Pour over mushrooms. Bake at 350° F for 1 hour or until puffed and lightly browned. Makes 4 to 6 servings.

To Microwave: Cook on high power (100%) 4 minutes, stirring twice. Cook 12 to 13 minutes more, stirring and rotating dish ½ turn after 4 minutes.

EGGS SARDOU

Croissants have become an everyday, any-occasion menu item. They are available in frozen form from **SARA LEE**, which makes them very convenient to find.

4 frozen **SARA LEE All-Butter Croissants**

1 package (10 ounces) frozen creamed spinach

4 poached eggs

  Hollandaise Sauce (see recipe)

Cut frozen croissants in half lengthwise; leave together. Heat frozen croissants on ungreased baking sheet in preheated 325° F oven 9 to 11 minutes. Cook spinach according to package directions. For each serving, spoon ¼ of creamed spinach over each croissant bottom half. Top with 1 poached egg. Spoon Hollandaise Sauce over egg. Top with remaining croissant half. Makes 4 servings.

HOLLANDAISE SAUCE

2 egg yolks

1 tablespoon lemon juice

½ cup (1 stick) butter, cut into 3 chunks

Mix egg yolks and lemon juice in a small saucepan until smooth. Over low heat, add butter, 1 piece at a time, stirring constantly until butter has melted. Continue stirring until mixture thickens. Makes 4 servings.

SPINACH STRATA

You won't believe how good this is until you try it. This dish can be used as a meatless main course, an appetizer or hors d'oeuvre, and it's inexpensive and easy to prepare. The RITZ® Crackers are the key to success.

72 RITZ® Crackers from 1 (12-ounce) box

10 ounces Muenster cheese, grated (2½ cups)

2 (10-ounce) packages frozen chopped spinach, thawed and well drained

2½ cups milk

5 eggs

2 tablespoons Dijon mustard

½ teaspoon liquid hot pepper seasoning

2 cloves garlic, crushed

In 2-quart shallow baking dish, arrange 24 RITZ Crackers slightly overlapping in 3 long rows. Combine cheese and spinach; spoon ⅓ over crackers; repeat crackers and cheese-mixture layers 2 more times.

In medium bowl, beat together milk, eggs, mustard, hot pepper seasoning, and garlic; pour over top layer of cheese mixture. Bake at 350° F for 30 to 35 minutes or until puffed and golden. Makes 6 servings.

SPINACH QUICHE

Attention TRISCUIT lovers! TRISCUIT® Wafers make a great tasting crust for this quiche. Use this crust with your other favorite quiche recipes, too. Quiche also makes a fine appetizer, side dish or main dish.

Crust:

35 **NABISCO TRISCUIT®** Wafers, finely
   crushed (about 1½ cups crumbs)
¼ cup BLUE BONNET® Margarine, melted

Filling:

2 tablespoons BLUE BONNET® Margarine
3 tablespoons minced onion
1 (10-ounce) package frozen, chopped
   spinach, thawed and well drained
3 eggs
1 cup light cream
½ cup cottage cheese
⅛ teaspoon ground black pepper

⅛ teaspoon ground nutmeg

4 ounces Swiss cheese, grated (about 1 cup)

1. Make Crust: Preheat oven to 300° F. In medium bowl, blend TRISCUIT Wafers crumbs with BLUE BONNET Margarine; press evenly onto bottom and sides of 9-inch pie plate. Bake 10 minutes; set aside.
2. Make Filling: Increase oven to 325° F. In medium skillet, over medium heat, melt BLUE BONNET Margarine; sauté onion about 2 minutes, or until tender. Stir in spinach; set aside.
3. In blender container, at low speed, combine eggs, cream, cottage cheese, pepper, and nutmeg for 30 seconds.
4. Sprinkle cheese in bottom of pie shell; top with spinach mixture; slowly pour egg mixture over spinach. Bake 45 minutes, or until set. Let stand 5 minutes before serving. Makes 6 servings.

FISH FILLET BAKE

Family and friends will love the taste of this colorful dish, which would be great to serve for luncheons or dinners.

¾ cup finely chopped onion

½ cup finely chopped celery

3 tablespoons oil

½ cup uncooked long-grain rice

¾ teaspoon garlic salt

⅛ teaspoon cayenne, if desired

3⅓ cups (two 14½-ounce cans)
    CONTADINA Stewed Tomatoes
1 pound white fish fillets
    Fresh parsley
    Lemon slices

Sauté onion and celery in oil in large skillet. Stir in rice and sauté until rice browns slightly. Add garlic salt, cayenne, and tomatoes. Mix well. Place fish in bottom of buttered 12 × 7½ × 2-inch baking dish. Pour rice mixture over fish. Cover with foil and bake in hot oven (400° F) 45 to 55 minutes or until rice is tender. Garnish with parsley and lemon slices. Makes 4 servings.

CURRIED SHRIMP FILLING (or Curried Tuna Filling)

This recipe tastes equally good if you substitute tuna for shrimp. This makes it less expensive and especially convenient when shrimp is unavailable.

4 frozen **SARA LEE** All-Butter Croissants
3 tablespoons butter
¼ cup chopped onion
¼ cup chopped celery
¾ teaspoon curry powder
¼ cup all-purpose flour
1½ cups half and half or milk
¼ teaspoon ground ginger
1 teaspoon lemon juice

⅓ cup light or dark raisins

10 ounces medium shrimp, cooked, *OR* 1 can (6½ ounces) tuna, drained and flaked

Chopped peanuts *OR* sliced green onion tops, optional

Cut frozen croissants in half lengthwise; leave together. Heat frozen croissants on ungreased baking sheet in preheated 325° F oven 9 to 11 minutes. Sauté onion and celery in butter. Stir in curry powder; cook 1 minute. Stir in flour; heat until bubbly. Stir in half and half, ginger, and lemon juice. Cook over low heat, stirring until thickened. Stir in raisins and shrimp. Heat 2 to 3 minutes longer. Serve spooned over croissant bottom halves. Garnish with peanuts, if desired. Top with remaining croissant halves. Makes 4 servings.

Breads

APPLE NUT BREAD

You'll be proud to serve this or bring it as a hostess gift.

  36 **WHEATSWORTH®** Stone Ground
     Wheat Crackers, finely rolled (about 1½
     cups crumbs)

1½ cups all-purpose flour

   1 cup sugar

   1 cup PLANTERS® Walnuts, chopped

   1 cup chopped apple

   1 cup milk

   3 eggs, slightly beaten

  ⅓ cup PLANTERS® Peanut Oil

   4 teaspoons baking powder

   2 teaspoons ground cinnamon

   2 teaspoons grated lemon peel

In large bowl, with electric mixer at medium speed, combine all ingredients until just blended, about ½ minute. Pour into greased and floured 9 × 5 × 3-inch loaf pan. Bake at 350° F for 1¼ hours, or until done. Cool in pan on wire rack 10 minutes. Remove from pan to cool completely. Makes one 9-inch loaf.

BANANA BREAD

By using **BUTTER BUDS** instead of butter in this recipe, you can cut down on calories and cholesterol.

       1 cup sifted all-purpose flour

    ¾ cup sifted whole-wheat flour

       2 teaspoons baking powder

    ¼ teaspoon baking soda

    ¼ teaspoon salt

       1 egg, well beaten

       1 packet **BUTTER BUDS,** mixed with ¼
          cup hot water

    ¼ cup sugar

       3 packets **SWEET 'N LOW**

       1 teaspoon vanilla

       1 cup mashed bananas

Preheat oven to 350° F. In medium-size bowl, sift together flours, baking powder, baking soda, and salt. In separate bowl, combine egg, BUTTER BUDS, sugar, SWEET 'N LOW, vanilla, and bananas. Add dry ingredients, mix until moist. Turn into nonstick 9 × 5-inch loaf pan. Bake 1 hour, or until toothpick inserted in center comes out clean. Serves 18.

GOLDEN CHEESE BREAD

   1 package active dry yeast

1½ cups lukewarm (105° F to 115° F) water

  ½ cup dry **CARNATION** Nonfat Dry Milk

   2 tablespoons sugar

   2 tablespoons oil

1½ teaspoons salt

3¾ to 4¼ cups flour

1½ cups (6 ounces) shredded Cheddar
     cheese

Dissolve yeast in warm water in large bowl. Stir in dry
nonfat milk, sugar, oil, and salt. Stir in about 3½ cups
flour to make a stiff dough. Turn out on floured surface.
Knead until smooth and elastic, working in additional
flour, about 8 minutes. Place in oiled bowl; turn to oil
top surface. Cover; let rise in warm place until doubled
in bulk, about 1 hour. Punch down. Turn out on lightly
floured board. Roll out to 12 × 14-inch rectangle. Sprinkle cheese over surface of dough. Roll starting at long
end; cut into 1-inch sections. Cut each section into
quarters. Divide the pieces of dough evenly between two
well oiled 8½ × 4½ × 2½-inch loaf dishes. Cover; let rise
in warm place until doubled in bulk, about 1 hour. Bake
in slow oven (325° F) 25 to 30 minutes. Remove from
pans; cool on wire racks. Makes 2 loaves.

COOKING TIP: Stirring CARNATION Nonfat Dry Milk into
dry ingredients eliminates the extra step of scalding
fresh milk. Loaves made with milk have a more velvety
grain, creamier white crumb, and browner crust than
those made without milk. Cheddar cheese is rolled
through this loaf for a special taste.

ENERGY BREAD

Freshly baked bread is a welcome accompaniment to any meal.

$\frac{1}{2}$ cup chopped dried apricots

$\frac{1}{2}$ cup raisins

$\frac{3}{4}$ cup plus 1 tablespoon whole-wheat flour, divided

$\frac{3}{4}$ cup all-purpose flour

$\frac{3}{4}$ cup firmly packed light brown sugar

$3\frac{1}{2}$ teaspoons baking powder

2 teaspoons cinnamon

$\frac{1}{2}$ teaspoon ground cloves

$\frac{1}{2}$ teaspoon salt

2 eggs

1 packet **BUTTER BUDS** made into liquid

$1\frac{1}{2}$ cups bran cereal

$\frac{3}{4}$ cup low-fat milk

Preheat oven to 350° F. Toss apricots and raisins with 1 tablespoon whole-wheat flour; set aside. In large bowl, thoroughly combine all-purpose flour, $\frac{3}{4}$ cup whole-wheat flour, sugar, baking powder, cinnamon, cloves, and salt. In separate bowl, combine remaining ingredients. Stir into flour mixture just until moistened. Stir in apricots and raisins. Turn batter into nonstick 9 × 5-inch loaf pan. Bake 1 hour, or until toothpick inserted in center comes out clean. Cool on wire rack 10 minutes. Remove from pan and cool completely. Makes 18 servings.

FIG NUT BREAD

If you love **FIG NEWTONS®** Cookies, you'll love this fruity recipe! It's excellent.

¾ cup milk, scalded

20 <u>FIG NEWTONS® Cookies</u>, broken

1½ cups sifted all-purpose flour

¼ teaspoon salt

¾ teaspoon baking soda

¼ cup BLUE BONNET® Margarine

¼ cup light brown sugar, firmly packed

1 teaspoon grated orange rind

2 eggs

1 cup nuts, coarsely chopped

Pour milk over FIG NEWTONS Cookies; let cool. Sift together next three ingredients. Cream BLUE BONNET Margarine, sugar, and orange rind. Add eggs, one at a time. Stir in sifted dry ingredients, nuts, and softened FIG NEWTONS Cookies. Pour into greased 9×5×3-inch loaf pan. Let stand 10 minutes. Bake in a preheated moderate oven (350° F) 50 to 55 minutes or until cake tester inserted in center comes out clean. Cool. Store wrapped in aluminum foil overnight. Slice thinly. Makes one 9-inch loaf.

PUMPKIN CRANBERRY NUT BREAD

This new, delightfully fresh-tasting quick bread features delicious pumpkin, fresh cranberries, and chunky nutmeats for a festive holiday brunch or snack. You'll love making and giving this beautiful bread this season—and for years to come.

    3½ cups flour
     2 teaspoons ground cinnamon
     1 teaspoon salt
     1 teaspoon baking soda
    ½ teaspoon baking powder
     2 teaspoons grated orange rind
     2 cups sugar
    ¾ cup butter or margarine, softened
     3 eggs
     1 can (16 ounces) **LIBBY'S Solid Pack Pumpkin**
     1 cup chopped walnuts
     1 cup chopped cranberries
       Icing, walnuts, cranberry; optional garnish

Preheat oven to 350° F. Combine dry ingredients; set aside. Cream butter and sugar. Add eggs one at a time, mixing after each addition. Alternate additions of pumpkin and dry ingredients. Stir in nuts and cranberries. Pour batter into 2 lightly greased 8½ × 4½ × 2½-inch loaf pans. Bake 60 to 65 minutes or until bread tests done. If desired, drizzle with icing (mix just enough cream or milk into confectioners' sugar to make a slightly runny consistency); garnish with walnut halves and a cranberry. Yields 2 loaves.

BEST-EVER MUFFINS

The name of this recipe says it all.

$1\frac{3}{4}$ cups unsifted all-purpose flour

2 tablespoons sugar

$2\frac{1}{2}$ teaspoons **CALUMET®** Baking Powder

$\frac{3}{4}$ teaspoon salt

1 egg, well beaten

$\frac{3}{4}$ cup milk

$\frac{1}{3}$ cup liquid shortening

Mix together flour with sugar, baking powder, and salt. Combine egg and milk and add all at once to flour mixture. Add shortening. Then stir *only* until dry ingredients are moistened. (Batter will be lumpy.) Spoon into greased muffin pans, filling each about two-thirds full. Bake at 400° F for 25 minutes.

SPUR-OF-THE-MOMENT MUFFINS

Add these muffins to your menu and you'll get lots of compliments.

    2 cups shreds of wheat bran cereal
    2 cups buttermilk
    2 eggs, slightly beaten
    1 can (1 pound 4 ounces) <u>DOLE Crushed Pineapple in Syrup</u>
  ½ cup butter, melted
 2½ cups flour
  ¾ cup dark brown sugar, firmly packed
    2 teaspoons salt
    2 teaspoons baking soda
    1 cup diced walnuts

Combine bran and buttermilk in a large bowl; let stand 5 minutes. Stir in eggs, undrained pineapple, and melted butter. In another bowl, blend together flour, brown sugar, salt, baking soda, and nuts. Add to bran mixture all at once. Stir until just mixed; batter will not be smooth. Spoon batter into greased muffin cups, making only the amount you need today. Bake in a 375° F oven about 25 minutes. Cover remaining batter and refrigerate up to 3 weeks, using as needed. Makes about 2 dozen.

Desserts:
Fabulous
Cakes,
No-Bake
and Bake Pies

CAKES

SPICY APPLE FIG CAKE

This interesting combination of ingredients combines to make this an inviting dessert that can be served anytime.

- ½ cup BLUE BONNET margarine
- 1 cup chunky applesauce
- 12 **FIG NEWTONS® Cookies,** crumbled
- 1 cup all-purpose flour
- 1 cup granulated sugar
- 1 teaspoon salt
- 1 teaspoon baking soda
- 1 teaspoon ground cinnamon
- ½ teaspoon ground nutmeg
- ¼ teaspoon ground cloves
- 1 cup chopped walnuts

In large saucepan, combine margarine and applesauce. Place over medium heat, stirring occasionally until melted, and combined. Remove from heat. Blend in 9 remaining ingredients, stirring until well blended. Pour batter into greased 9-cup Bundt pan. Bake in a preheated moderate oven (350° F) 55 to 60 minutes or until tester comes out clean. If desired, sprinkle with confectioners' sugar. Makes 10 (about 2½-inch) wedges.

BANANA SPLIT CAKE

Sensational—and easy, too.

Crust:

    2 cups graham cracker, chocolate wafer, or vanilla wafer crumbs

   ½ cup melted butter or margarine

Filling:

    2 envelopes **DREAM WHIP®** Whipped Topping Mix

    2 cups *cold* milk

    1 package (4-serving size) **JELL-O®** Brand Vanilla Flavor Instant Pudding and Pie Filling

    3 cups sliced bananas (about 4 medium)

    1 can (20 ounces) crushed pineapple in juice, drained

Combine crumbs and butter; press firmly on bottom of 13 × 9-inch pan. Bake at 375° F for about 8 minutes; then cool thoroughly. (Or chill for 1 hour.)

    Prepare whipped topping mix with 1 cup of the

milk as directed on package. Measure 2½ cups and set aside. Add remaining 1 cup milk and the pudding mix to remaining whipped topping. Blend; then beat at high speed of electric mixer for 2 minutes, scraping bowl occasionally. Spoon pudding mixture over crust. Arrange banana slices on pudding; spoon pineapple evenly over bananas. Spread measured whipped topping evenly over the fruit. Chill at least 4 hours. Garnish as desired. Makes 12 servings.

CARROT COCONUT CAKE

This cake is a real taste pleaser—BAKER'S® ANGEL FLAKE® Coconut gives it its unbelievable moistness.

       2 cups unsifted all-purpose flour

    2½ teaspoons baking soda

       2 teaspoons cinnamon

       1 teaspoon salt

       1 cup oil

       2 cups sugar

       3 eggs

       1 can (8 ounces) crushed pineapple in
          juice

       2 cups grated carrots

    1⅓ cups (about) **BAKER'S® ANGEL
          FLAKE®** or Premium Shred Coconut

      ½ cup chopped nuts

Combine flour, baking soda, cinnamon, and salt. Beat oil, sugar, and eggs until well blended. Add flour mixture and beat until smooth. Blend in pineapple with juice, carrots, coconut, and nuts. Pour into greased 10-inch tube pan.* Bake at 350° F for 55 minutes, or until cake tester inserted in center comes out clean. Cool in pan 10 minutes. Remove from pan and finish cooling on rack. Frost with Coconut Cream Cheese Frosting.

Coconut Cream Cheese Frosting: Sauté 1 cup BAKER'S® ANGEL FLAKE® Coconut in 1½ tablespoons butter until golden brown, stirring constantly. Remove from heat; spread on absorbent paper and cool. Cream 1 package (3 ounces) cream cheese, softened, with ¼ cup butter or margarine until smooth. Add 3 cups sifted confectioners' sugar alternately with 1 tablespoon milk and ½ teaspoon vanilla; beat until smooth. Add half the coconut; spread on cake and sprinkle with remaining coconut. Makes about 2½ cups.

In high altitude areas, increase flour to 2¼ cups; reduce baking soda to 2¼ teaspoons, sugar to 1¾ cups, and oil to ¾ cup; add 1 tablespoon water with the eggs.

*Cake may be baked in a 13×9-inch pan for 50 to 55 minutes.

AMARETTO CHEESECAKE

Savor the flavor of this wonderful cheesecake dessert. Use versatile NILLA® Wafers to make crusts for other fillings, too.

Crust:

50 **NILLA**® Wafers, finely rolled (about 2 cups crumbs)

⅓ cup sugar

½ cup finely chopped PLANTERS® Almonds

½ cup BLUE BONNET® Margarine, melted

Filling:

3 (8-ounce) packages cream cheese, softened

⅔ cup sugar

1 cup dairy sour cream

4 eggs

½ cup amaretto liqueur

Garnish:

2 kiwi fruit, peeled, sliced and halved

Combine NILLA® Wafer crumbs, ⅓ cup sugar, PLANT-ERS® Almonds, and BLUE BONNET® Margarine; press against bottom and 2-inches up sides of a 9-inch springform pan. Set aside.

Beat together cream cheese and ⅔ cup sugar until smooth; blend in sour cream, eggs, and amaretto. Pour into prepared crust. Bake at 350° F for 1 hour. Turn oven off and allow cheesecake to remain in oven 30 minutes, leaving door slightly ajar. Cool; chill 4 hours or until serving time. Garnish with kiwi slices. Makes 12 servings.

BEAT-THE-HEAT CHEESECAKE

The easiest, creamiest, dreamiest cheesecake ever! For special occasions, top with fresh strawberries or blueberries.

   2 envelopes __KNOX Unflavored Gelatine__
 ¾ cup sugar
   1 cup boiling water
   1 cup creamed cottage cheese
   2 packages (8 ounces each) cream cheese, softened
   1 cup (½ pint) whipping or heavy cream
   1 tablespoon vanilla extract
   2 teaspoons grated lemon peel
     Graham Cracker Almond Crust (see recipe)

In large bowl, mix unflavored gelatine with ¼ cup sugar; add boiling water and stir until gelatine is completely dissolved. With electric mixer, add remaining ingredients, one at a time, beating well after each addition. Turn into prepared crust; chill until firm. Garnish, if desired, with almonds and fruit. Makes about 12 servings.

Graham Cracker Almond Crust: In small bowl, combine 1 cup graham cracker crumbs, ½ cup ground almonds, 2 tablespoons sugar, ¼ cup melted butter or margarine, and ½ teaspoon almond extract. Press onto bottom and sides of 9-inch springform pan; chill.

FROZEN MOCHA CHEESECAKE

This is a very special cheesecake with the perfect mocha taste. Try it once and you'll make it often.

1¼ cups chocolate wafer cookie crumbs (about 24 cookies)

¼ cup sugar

¼ cup margarine or butter, melted

1 (8-ounce) package cream cheese, softened

1 (14-ounce) EAGLE® Brand Sweetened Condensed Milk (NOT evaporated milk)

⅔ cup chocolate-flavored syrup

2 tablespoons instant coffee

1 teaspoon hot water

1 cup (½ pint) whipping cream, whipped

Additional chocolate crumbs (optional)

In small bowl, combine crumbs, sugar, and margarine. In buttered 9-inch springform pan or 13 × 9-inch baking dish, pat crumbs firmly on bottom and up sides of pan. Chill. In large mixer bowl, beat cheese until fluffy; add EAGLE Brand and chocolate syrup. In small bowl, dissolve coffee in water; add to EAGLE Brand mixture. Mix well. Fold in whipped cream. Pour into prepared pan. Cover. Freeze 6 hours or until firm. Garnish with additional chocolate crumbs, if desired. Return leftovers to freezer. Makes one 9-inch cheesecake.

PUMPKIN CHEESECAKE

Don't wait for a special occasion to enjoy this great cheese-cake.

1 (16-ounce) package **FIG NEWTONS®**
Cookies

1 (8-ounce) package cream cheese,
softened

¾ cup light brown sugar, firmly packed

1⅛ teaspoons ground cinnamon

1 (16-ounce) can solid pack pumpkin

3 eggs, separated

½ teaspoon ground nutmeg

½ teaspoon salt

½ cup heavy cream

Grease bottom and sides of a 9-inch springform pan; arrange 16 FIG NEWTONS Cookies around edge, filling side touching. Cut remaining FIG NEWTONS Cookies in half crosswise and arrange over bottom. Beat cream cheese in large bowl of electric mixer until fluffy. Add ½ cup brown sugar, 1 teaspoon cinnamon, pumpkin, egg yolks, nutmeg, and salt; beat until well blended. Beat egg whites until soft peaks form; gradually add remaining brown sugar and continue beating until stiff. Fold into pumpkin mixture. Pour into prepared pan. Bake in preheated moderate oven (350° F) about 1 hour and 10 minutes or until knife inserted midway between edge and center comes out clean. Cool completely and remove rim. Whip cream with remaining cinnamon until stiff; serve with cheesecake. Makes 12 (about 2-inch) wedges.

SPICY FRUIT CRISP

This is a delicious and easy recipe. Serve it to the whole family for dessert and as an after-school snack for kids.

12 **NABISCO** Pecan Shortbread Cookies, crushed (about 1⅔ cups crumbs)

2 tablespoons light brown sugar

1½ teaspoons ground cinnamon

½ teaspoon ground nutmeg

¼ cup BLUE BONNET® Margarine, softened

4 medium baking apples, sliced (about 4 cups)

Whipped cream or ice cream

In small bowl, combine NABISCO Pecan Shortbread Cookie crumbs, brown sugar, cinnamon, and nutmeg. Using pastry blender or fork, cut in BLUE BONNET Margarine until mixture resembles coarse crumbs. Arrange fruit in greased 9-inch square pan. Sprinkle crumb mixture evenly over fruit. Bake at 375° F for 30 to 35 minutes. Serve warm topped with whipped cream or ice cream. Makes 6 servings.

Busy Cooks' Variation: In place of apples, substitute 2 (16-ounce) cans drained fruit (sliced peaches, pears, or mixed fruit). Any combination can be used.

MARBLED 1-2-3-4 CAKE

Marbled cakes are always so appealing to the eye. This one tastes great, too.

1 package (4 ounces) **BAKER'S®**
GERMAN'S® Sweet Chocolate

1 cup butter or margarine

2 cups sugar

3 cups sifted **SWANS DOWN®** Cake Flour

3 teaspoons **CALUMET®** Baking Powder

½ teaspoon salt

4 eggs

1 cup milk

1 teaspoon vanilla

½ teaspoon almond extract

Melt chocolate in saucepan over low heat; set aside. Cream butter. Gradually add sugar, beating until light and fluffy. (Beat 10 minutes with an electric mixer, or longer by hand.) Sift flour with baking powder and salt. Add eggs, one at a time, beating well after each addition. Add flour mixture alternately with milk and flavorings, beating until smooth after each addition. Pour half the batter into a greased and floured 10-inch tube pan. Fold chocolate into remaining batter; spoon over plain batter. (Chocolate batter goes to bottom during baking for a marbled effect.) Bake at 350° F for about 1 hour and 10 minutes, or until cake tester inserted into center comes out clean. Cool in pan 15 minutes. Remove from pan and finish cooling on rack.

MOCHA RUM TORTE

Save time and energy by using SARA LEE Pound Cake to make this extra special treat with a sophisticated taste.

  1 package (6 ounces) semi-sweet chocolate chips

½ cup dairy sour cream

¾ teaspoon instant coffee powder

  1 frozen **SARA LEE Pound Cake,** thawed

  1 tablespoon rum

  3 tablespoons apricot preserves

    Whole pecans *or* hazelnuts

Melt chocolate in small bowl 1 to 2 minutes in microwave oven *or* over low heat; cool slightly. Stir in sour cream and coffee powder. Cut Pound Cake lengthwise into 3 layers. Spread about ¼ cup chocolate mixture on bottom cake layer. Top with middle layer; sprinkle with rum. Spread with about ¼ cup chocolate mixture, then apricot preserves. Replace cake top. Spread remaining chocolate mixture over cake top and sides. Decorate with pecans. Chill. Makes 10 to 12 servings.

Microwave Hint: Pound cake slices take about 10 seconds to thaw. Whole cake takes about 1 minute to thaw.

TRIFLE

SARA LEE Pound Cake makes it so convenient to prepare delicious desserts. This trifle is a splendid example.

    1 frozen **SARA LEE Pound Cake,** thawed
 ¼ cup sherry *or* orange liqueur *or* orange
    juice
 ½ cup strawberry preserves
    2 cups vanilla pudding *or* custard
    2 cups fresh *or* canned fruit*
    Whipped cream, optional

Cut pound cake into 10 slices; cut each slice into 8 cubes. Place ½ of cubes in 2½-quart glass bowl; sprinkle with ½ of sherry. Spoon ½ of preserves over cubes, then layer on ½ of pudding and ½ of fruit. Repeat with remaining pound cake, sherry, preserves, pudding, and fruit. Chill, covered, to blend flavors 2 hours before serving. Garnish with whipped cream, if desired. Makes 15 to 18 servings.

*Fresh fruit—sliced strawberries, bananas, or peaches.
Canned fruit—Mandarin oranges or crushed pineapple.

NO-BAKE PIES

BANANA CREAM PIE

This is a heavenly cream pie. It tastes fantastic but is so easy to prepare.

> 1 banana
> 1 prepared 9-inch graham cracker crumb crust
> 1 package (6-serving size) JELL-O® Brand Instant Pudding and Pie Filling, banana cream or vanilla flavor
> 2 cups *cold* milk
> 1 container (4 ounces) BIRDS EYE® COOL WHIP® Non-Dairy Whipped Topping, thawed

1. Slice banana into pie shell. Prepare pie filling mix as directed on package for pie, reducing milk to 2 cups.
2. Fold in half of the whipped topping.
3. Spoon over banana in shell. Chill at least 1 hour. Garnish with remaining whipped topping.

COCONUT CUSTARD PIE

Custard fans will love this pie. It is easy to prepare using JELL-O® Brand AMERICANA® Golden Egg Custard Mix.

> 1 package (3 ounces) JELL-O® Brand AMERICANA® Golden Egg Custard Mix
>
> 2 cups milk
>
> 1 egg yolk (optional)
>
> ⅔ cup BAKER'S® ANGEL FLAKE® Coconut*
>
> 1 baked 8-inch pie shell, cooled

Blend custard mix with milk in saucepan; add egg yolk. Bring quickly to a boil, stirring constantly. (Mixture will be thin.) Remove from heat. Cool 15 minutes, stirring often. Sprinkle coconut in bottom of pie shell. Pour custard mixture over coconut. Chill 3 hours. Garnish with additional coconut, toasted, if desired. Refrigerate any leftover pie. Makes one 8-inch pie.

*Or use ½ cup coarsely chopped pecans; garnish with additional nuts, if desired.

FRUITED SOUR CREAM PIE

Here is a dessert that everyone will love.

  1 can (16 ounces) fruit cocktail*

  1 package (3 ounces) **JELL-O**® Brand **Gelatin,** any flavor

  1 envelope **DREAM WHIP**® Whipped **Topping Mix**

 ½ cup milk

 ½ cup (½ pint) sour cream

  1 baked 9-inch pie shell

Drain fruit, reserving ⅔ cup of the syrup. Bring measured syrup to a boil in saucepan. Add gelatin and stir until dissolved. Chill 10 minutes. Prepare whipped topping mix with milk as directed on package. Blend in sour cream. Reduce mixer speed to low and blend in gelatin. Chill, if necessary, until mixture will mound. Fold in fruit; spoon into pie shell. Chill at least 4 hours. Garnish with additional fruit, if desired. Makes one 9-inch pie.

    *Or use 1 can (16 ounces) apricot or peach halves; dice fruit before folding into gelatin.

10 MINUTE GERMAN SWEET CHOCOLATE PIE

This is a really fantastic pie that is very easy to prepare. It will melt in your mouth.

1 package (4 ounces) **BAKER'S® GERMAN'S® Sweet Chocolate**

⅓ cup milk

2 tablespoons sugar (optional)

1 package (3 ounces) cream cheese, softened

3½ cups or 1 container (8 ounces) **BIRDS EYE® COOL WHIP® Non-Dairy Whipped Topping,** thawed

1 prepared 8-inch graham-cracker crumb crust

Heat chocolate and 2 tablespoons of the milk in saucepan over low heat, stirring until chocolate is melted. Beat sugar into cream cheese; add remaining milk and chocolate mixture and beat until smooth. Fold chocolate mixture into whipped topping, blending until smooth. Spoon into crust. Freeze until firm, about 4 hours. Garnish with chocolate curls, if desired. Store any leftover pie in freezer.

ICE CREAM SUNDAE PIE

This is a refreshingly cool dessert that the OREO® Chocolate Sandwich Cookies crust makes very special.

Crust:

¼ cup BLUE BONNET® Margarine

25 OREO® Chocolate Sandwich Cookies, crushed

1 teaspoon ground cinnamon

Filling:

1 quart coffee or vanilla ice cream, slightly softened

¾ cup semi-sweet chocolate pieces

¼ cup BLUE BONNET Margarine

1 tablespoon coffee-flavored liqueur (optional)

1 teaspoon milk

Garnish:

1 cup heavy cream, whipped

1. Make Crust: In medium saucepan, over low heat, melt margarine; remove from heat; stir in OREO crumbs and ground cinnamon. Press evenly onto bottom and sides of 9-inch pie plate, refrigerate 15 minutes.

2. Make Filling: Spread ½ ice cream evenly into prepared crust. Freeze until firm, about 15 minutes. In
   small saucepan, over low heat, melt chocolate pieces
   and margarine; remove from heat. If desired, stir in
   liqueur.
3. Remove pie from freezer; quickly spread ⅔ chocolate
   mixture over ice cream. Cover with remaining ice
   cream. Stir milk into remaining chocolate mixture,
   drizzle over ice cream. Freeze until firm, 2 to 3 hours.
4. To Serve: Top with whipped cream. Makes 8 servings.

NESSELRO PIE

You'll feel so good when this elegant-looking pie gets raves
from guests.

    1 envelope unflavored gelatin
   ⅛ teaspoon salt
    2 tablespoons sugar
    3 eggs, separated
    1 cup milk
   ½ cup heavy cream, whipped
   ¾ cup **RAFFETTO** Nesselro
    1 9-inch baked pie shell

Combine gelatin, salt, and sugar. In top part of double boiler beat egg yolks. Stir in milk and gelatin mixture. Cook over hot, not boiling, water, stirring occasionally, until mixture coats a spoon and thickens slightly. Refrigerate, stirring occasionally, until mixture mounds when dropped from a spoon. Beat until just smooth. Beat egg whites just until stiff. Fold into custard with whipped cream. Fold in Nesselro and turn into baked pie shell. Chill until set. Garnish with more whipped cream and shaved chocolate, if desired. Makes one 9-inch pie.

STRAWBERRY YOGURT PIE

This yogurt pie is a little tangy, a little sweet, and very refreshing.

    2 cups DANNON Strawberry Yogurt
    ½ cup crushed strawberries
    1 container (8 ounces) thawed COOL
       WHIP® Non-Dairy Whipped Topping
    1 prepared 8- or 9-inch graham cracker
       pie crust

Thoroughly combine crushed fruit and yogurt in bowl. Fold in COOL WHIP, blending well. Spoon into crust and freeze about 4 hours. Remove from freezer and place in refrigerator 30 minutes (or longer for softer texture) before serving. Store any leftover pie in freezer. Makes one 8- or 9-inch pie.

PUMPKIN PECAN CHIFFON PIE

A delightful dessert! Be prepared to dish out seconds. Use this easy crust made with NABISCO® Pecan Shortbread Cookies for other pie recipes, too.

Crust:

  22 <u>NABISCO Pecan Shortbread Cookies</u>

  ¼ cup BLUE BONNET® Margarine, melted

Filling:

   3 eggs, separated, at room temperature

  ¾ cup light brown sugar

  ¾ cup milk

   1 envelope unflavored gelatin

   1 cup canned or cooked fresh pumpkin

  ¼ teaspoon salt

   1 teaspoon ground cinnamon

  ¼ teaspoon ground ginger

  ¼ teaspoon ground nutmeg

  ¼ cup sugar

   2 cups whipped cream

Finely roll 12 NABISCO Pecan Shortbread Cookies; mix in melted BLUE BONNET Margarine. Press onto bottom of 8-inch springform pan. Use remaining 10 NABISCO Pecan Shortbread Cookies to line sides of pan; set aside.

In medium saucepan, combine egg yolks, brown sugar, milk, and gelatin; heat over low heat, stirring constantly, until gelatin dissolves. Remove from heat;

stir in pumpkin, salt, and spices. Chill until partially set. Beat egg whites, gradually adding sugar, until stiff peaks form; fold into pumpkin mixture. Fold in 1 cup whipped cream. Pour into prepared pan. Chill 2 to 3 hours or until firm. Remove sides of pan. Garnish with remaining whipped cream. Makes 10 servings.

NO-BAKE FRUITED CHEESE DESSERT

This do-ahead, no-bake dessert will be a sure hit, anytime.

1 6-ounce package (1⅔ cups) **SUN-MAID Fruit Bits**

1 cup apple juice

1 8-ounce package cream cheese, softened

1⅓ cups milk

1 package (4-serving size) lemon flavor instant pudding and pie filling mix

1 9-inch prepared graham cracker pie shell

In a medium saucepan, combine fruit bits and juice; bring to a boil. Reduce heat and simmer until fruit absorbs juice. Cool. Beat cream cheese until smooth, slowly beat in milk. Add pudding mix; beat until smooth and thickened. Fold in fruit bits and spoon into pie shell. Chill. Makes 8 servings.

BAKE PIES

APRICOT PINEAPPLE PIE

Apricots and pineapples are a fantastic combination. Especially so in this pie which makes a perfect ending to a lovely dinner.

    1 8¼-ounce can crushed pineapple,
       undrained
    ⅔ cup granulated sugar
    2 teaspoons corn starch
    1 tablespoon butter or margarine
1½ cups drained, cooked **SUN-MAID or
       SUNSWEET Dried Apricots,** cut in
       quarters
    1 8-inch unbaked pastry shell and strips
       for lattice top*

*Recipe for 9-inch pie shell is enough for 8-inch shell
and lattice strips.

In a medium saucepan, combine pineapple, sugar, corn starch, and butter. Heat to boiling, stirring often; remove from heat and stir in apricots. Turn into pastry-lined 8-inch pie pan. Top with lattice pastry strips. Flute edge, building up a rim. Bake at 425° F for 35 to 40 minutes or until well browned. Cool before cutting. Makes one 8-inch pie.

Pastry Squares: Use pastry for 2 crust 9-inch pie shell. On a lightly floured board, roll out pastry to a 12 × 18-inch rectangle. Cut dough in half on the 12-inch side and make 2 cuts, 6 inches apart, on the 18-inch side. Makes six 6-inch squares.

CHERRY COBBLER

The kids will love this marvelous recipe and you will, too!

2 cans (16 ounces each) water-packed pitted red sour cherries*

1 to 1¼ cups sugar

¼ cup **MINUTE**® Tapioca

¼ teaspoon salt

2 tablespoons butter or margarine

¼ cup water

1 cup biscuit mix

Drain cherries, reserving 1½ cups liquid. Combine sugar, tapioca, and salt in saucepan; add cherries and measured liquid. Let stand 5 minutes. Bring just to a boil over medium heat, stirring constantly. Pour into greased 9-inch square pan or a 2-quart baking dish;

dot with butter. Stir water into biscuit mix and drop from teaspoon onto hot cherry mixture. Bake at 425° F for 20 to 25 minutes. Serve warm, with cream, if desired. Makes 8 servings.

*Or use syrup-packed cherries and reduce sugar to ¾ cup.

CHOCOLATE ANGEL PIE

The Quick Coconut Crust made with BAKER'S® ANGEL FLAKE® Coconut gives a special appeal to this easy and delicious pie. Try it and make it a part of your permanent recipe collection of family favorites.

1 package (4 ounces) BAKER'S® GERMAN'S® Sweet Chocolate

2 tablespoons water

2 cups thawed BIRDS EYE® COOL WHIP® Non-Dairy Whipped Topping

1 baked 8-inch Quick Coconut Crust, cooled (see recipe)

Heat chocolate with water in saucepan over low heat, stirring until chocolate is melted. Cool until thickened. Blend whipped topping into melted chocolate. Spoon into Quick Coconut Crust and chill at least 2 hours. Garnish with additional whipped topping and chocolate curls, if desired.

QUICK COCONUT CRUST

$\frac{1}{4}$ cup butter or margarine, melted

2 cups **BAKER'S® ANGEL FLAKE®** or
Premium Shred Coconut

Combine butter and coconut. Evenly press into an ungreased 8-inch pie pan. Bake at 300° F for 20 to 30 minutes, or until golden brown. Cool.

FUDGY PECAN PIE

A delightful, easy, delicious dessert from the Borden kitchens that will be a favorite in your kitchen, too.

1 9-inch unbaked pastry shell

1 (4-ounce) package sweet cooking
chocolate *or* 2 (1-ounce) squares
unsweetened chocolate

$\frac{1}{4}$ cup margarine or butter

1 (14-ounce) can **EAGLE®** Brand
Sweetened Condensed Milk (NOT
evaporated milk)

$\frac{1}{2}$ cup hot water

2 eggs, well beaten

1 teaspoon vanilla extract

$\frac{1}{8}$ teaspoon salt

$1\frac{1}{4}$ cups pecan halves or pieces

Preheat oven to 350° F. In medium saucepan, over low heat, melt chocolate and margarine. Stir in EAGLE® Brand, hot water, and eggs; *mix well*. Remove from heat; stir in remaining ingredients (or reserve 1 cup pecans to arrange on top). Pour into prepared pastry shell. (Top with reserved pecans). Bake 40 to 45 minutes or until center is set. Cool. Chill 3 hours. Garnish as desired. Refrigerate leftovers. Makes one 9-inch pie.

PUMPKIN PIE

Enjoy traditional Pumpkin Pie all year through. It's easy to make and a real favorite. The smooth custard filling goes together quickly and easily. Serve it with coffee anytime—any day of the year.

        2 slightly beaten eggs
    1½ cups canned pumpkin
        1 cup sugar
      ½ teaspoon salt
        1 teaspoon cinnamon
      ¼ teaspoon ginger
      ¼ teaspoon cloves
      ¼ teaspoon nutmeg
    1½ cups undiluted **CARNATION**
        Evaporated Milk
        9-inch unbaked pie shell

Combine eggs, pumpkin, sugar, salt, and spices. Gradually add evaporated milk. Mix well. Pour into unbaked pie shell. Bake in hot oven (400° F) 15 minutes; reduce oven temperature to 350° F and continue baking about 40 minutes, or until knife inserted near center of pie comes out clean. Cool before serving. (Filling will firm up while cooling.) Makes one 9-inch pie.

FRUIT COCKTAIL CREAM PIE

DEL MONTE Fruit Cocktail, a dessert by itself, is so convenient to keep on hand as a wonderful ingredient to make many recipes special.

Crust:

1½ cups graham cracker crumbs

¼ cup sugar

⅓ cup butter or margarine, melted

1 teaspoon grated lemon peel

Filling:

2 cups sour cream

⅔ cup sugar

1 teaspoon lemon juice

1 teaspoon vanilla extract

1 can (17 ounces) **DEL MONTE®** Fruit Cocktail, drained

Combine crumbs, ¼ cup sugar, butter, and lemon peel. Reserve 2 tablespoons mixture; press remaining mixture on bottom and sides (1½ inches high) of buttered 8-inch springform pan.

Combine sour cream, ⅔ cup sugar, lemon juice, and vanilla. Remove cherries from fruit for garnish. Fold remaining fruit into sour-cream mixture. Pour into crust. Top with reserved crumbs. Bake at 350° F, 20 to 25 minutes or until set. Garnish with reserved cherries and mint, if desired. Chill. Makes 8 to 10 servings.

WHEAT & RAISIN CHEESE PIE

Serve this delicious pie and enjoy its excellent texture and flavor combination.

3 cups <u>SHREDDED WHEAT TOASTED WHEAT & RAISINS,</u> finely rolled (1⅔ cups crumbs)

⅓ cup finely chopped PLANTERS® Walnuts

2 tablespoons firmly packed light brown sugar

6 tablespoons BLUE BONNET® Margarine, melted

1 8-ounce package cream cheese, softened

2 eggs

⅓ cup sugar

3 tablespoons lemon juice

1 cup nondairy whipped topping

In medium bowl combine SHREDDED WHEAT TOASTED WHEAT & RAISINS, PLANTERS Walnuts, and brown sugar; stir in melted BLUE BONNET Margarine. Press firmly on bottom and sides of greased 9-inch pie plate. Bake at 350° F for 10 minutes. Place on rack to cool. In medium bowl, using electric mixer at medium speed, beat cream cheese until light and fluffy. Add eggs, one at a time, beating after each. Blend in sugar and lemon juice; pour into cooled pie shell. Bake at 350° F for 15 to 20 minutes until nearly firm. Place on rack to cool. Chill several hours or overnight. Spread with whipped topping to serve. Makes 8 to 10 servings.

FAVORITE LEMON MERINGUE PIE

This is a frequently requested recipe favorite according to the people who make ARGO® and KINGSFORD'S® Corn Starch. It is so easy to prepare, so delicious, and looks so good. You'll love it.

 1 baked 9-inch pastry shell

1⅓ cups sugar

 3 tablespoons **ARGO® or KINGSFORD'S®**
  Corn Starch

1½ cups cold water

 3 egg yolks, slightly beaten
  Grated rind of 1 lemon

 ¼ cup lemon juice

 1 tablespoon margarine

 3 egg whites

In saucepan mix 1 cup of the sugar and corn starch. Gradually stir in water until smooth; stir in egg yolks. Bring to boil over medium heat, stirring constantly, and boil 1 minute. Remove from heat. Stir in next 3 ingredients; cool; turn into baked pastry shell. Beat egg whites until foamy. Gradually beat in ⅓ cup sugar; continue beating until stiff peaks form. Spread over filling, sealing to edge of crust. Bake in 350° F oven 15 minutes or until golden. Cool. Makes one 9-inch pie.

ARGO, KINGSFORD'S are registered trademarks of CPC International Inc.

COOKIES

BEACON HILL BROWNIES

Rich and delicious!

    1 package (8 squares) **BAKER'S®** Unsweetened Chocolate
    1 cup butter or margarine
    5 eggs
    3 cups sugar
    1 tablespoon vanilla
1½ cups flour
    2 cups coarsely chopped walnuts

Melt chocolate and butter in saucepan over very low heat, stirring constantly until smooth. Cool slightly. Beat eggs, sugar, and vanilla in large mixer bowl at high speed for 10 minutes. Blend in chocolate mixture at low speed. Add flour, beating just to blend; stir in walnuts. Spread in greased 13 × 9-inch pan. Bake at 375° F for 35 to 40 minutes. (Do not overbake.) Cool in pan; cut into squares. Makes 24 to 32 brownies.

Mint-Glazed Brownies: Prepare and bake Beacon Hill Brownies as directed. While still hot, place about 2 dozen thin chocolate-coated after-dinner mints on top of brownies. Return to oven for about 3 minutes. Then spread softened mints evenly over brownies. Cool in pan on rack; cut into squares or bars.

Nut-Topped Brownies: Prepare Beacon Hill Brownies as directed, omitting walnuts in the batter and sprinkling ½ cup coarsely chopped walnuts over batter in pan. Bake as directed and cool in pan. Melt 1 square BAKER'S® Unsweetened or Semi-Sweet Chocolate with 1 teaspoon butter or margarine, in saucepan over very low heat. Drizzle over brownies; let stand until chocolate is firm. Cut into squares or bars while still warm.

LIBBY'S GREAT PUMPKIN COOKIE RECIPE

America's new favorite—everyone will love Pumpkin Cookies!

- 4 cups unsifted all-purpose flour
- 2 cups quick or old-fashioned oats, uncooked
- 2 teaspoons baking soda
- 2 teaspoons ground cinnamon
- 1 teaspoon salt
- 1½ cups butter or margarine, softened
- 2 cups firmly packed brown sugar
- 1 cup granulated sugar
- 1 egg
- 1 teaspoon vanilla extract
- 1 can (16 ounces) **LIBBY'S Solid Pack Pumpkin**
- 1 cup real semi-sweet chocolate morsels

  Assorted icings or peanut butter

  Assorted candies, raisins or nuts

Preheat oven to 350° F. Combine flour, oats, soda, cinnamon, and salt; set aside. Cream butter; gradually add sugars, beating until light and fluffy. Add egg and vanilla; mix well. Alternate additions of dry ingredients and pumpkin, mixing well after each addition. Stir in morsels. For each cookie, drop ¼ cup dough onto lightly greased cookie sheet; spread into pumpkin shape using a thin metal spatula. Add a bit more dough to form stem. Bake at 350° F, 20 to 25 minutes, until cookies are firm and lightly browned. Remove from cookie sheets; cool on racks. Decorate using icing or peanut butter to affix assorted candies, raisins, or nuts. Yields about 32 large cookies.

Variation: Substitute 1 cup raisins for morsels.

Note: Dough may be frozen in an air-tight container. Thaw in refrigerator; bake as directed.

APRICOT COFFEE NUGGETS

These are delicious cookies that the whole family will love and request often.

½ cup butter or margarine, softened

1 cup brown sugar, packed

2 eggs

2 teaspoons instant coffee granules

¼ cup milk

1⅔ cups all-purpose flour

1 teaspoon salt

½ teaspoon baking powder

1 teaspoon cinnamon

1 cup chopped DIAMOND® Walnuts

1 cup chopped SUN-MAID or SUNSWEET Dried Apricots

Cream together butter and sugar. Beat in eggs one at a time (mixture will appear curdled). Dissolve instant coffee in milk. Sift together flour, salt, baking powder, and cinnamon; add to creamed mixture alternately with coffee mixture. Stir in walnuts and apricots; mix well. Drop by tablespoonfuls onto greased baking sheet. Bake at 375° F about 10 minutes, or until top springs back when touched lightly. Remove to wire rack to cool. Makes 36 cookies.

Note: To chop dried fruits (apricots) coat knife lightly with vegetable oil to prevent sticking; repeat if necessary.

CHOCOLATE CHUNK COOKIES

Enjoy these truly delectable home-baked cookies.

    2 cups unsifted all-purpose flour
    1 teaspoon baking soda
    ¾ teaspoon salt
    8 squares BAKER'S® Semi-Sweet
       Chocolate, coarsely chopped
    1 cup butter or margarine, softened
    ¾ cup firmly packed dark brown sugar
    ½ cup granulated sugar
    1 teaspoon vanilla
    1 egg
    ¼ cup sour cream
    1 cup coarsely chopped nuts*

*Or use 1 cup POST® GRAPE-NUTS® Brand Cereal.

Mix flour with baking soda and salt. Cut chocolate into large chunks. Cream butter. Gradually beat in sugars and continue beating until light and fluffy, about 5 minutes. Blend in vanilla, egg, and sour cream. Gradually add flour mixture, beating until smooth. Stir in nuts and the chocolate. Using scant ¼ cup for each, drop onto ungreased baking sheets, 2 inches apart. Bake at 375° F for 12 minutes or until lightly browned. Carefully remove from sheets; cool on racks. Makes 2 dozen large cookies.

GERMAN'S® SWEET CHOCOLATE CHUNK COOKIES

This is a winning recipe, special for everyday snacking or as a party pleaser. Make extra batches to share with drop-in guests. It's a chocolate lover's delight.

    1 cup unsifted all-purpose flour

    ½ teaspoon baking soda

    ½ teaspoon salt

    ½ cup butter or other shortening

    ½ cup granulated sugar

    ¼ cup firmly packed brown sugar

    1 egg

    1 teaspoon vanilla

    1 package (4 ounces) **BAKER'S®**

    GERMAN'S® Sweet Chocolate, diced

    ½ cup chopped nuts*

*Or use 1⅓ cups (about) **BAKER'S® ANGEL FLAKE®** Coconut.

Mix flour with soda and salt. Cream butter. Beat in sugars, egg, and vanilla and beat until light and fluffy. Blend in flour mixture. Add chocolate and nuts. Drop from teaspoon onto ungreased baking sheets, about 2 inches apart. Bake at 375° F for 8 to 10 minutes, or until lightly browned. Makes about 4 dozen.

Note: Recipe may be doubled or tripled. To dice chocolate easily, keep at 80° F to 90° F for 5 to 10 minutes.

For Jumbo Cookies: Measure ¼ cup dough for each and flatten slightly; bake 4 or 5 at a time on baking sheet; bake 12 to 14 minutes and let cool 1 to 2 minutes before removing from sheet; makes 12. *Or,* use 2 tablespoons dough for each cookie and bake 13 minutes; makes about 24 large cookies.

SUN-MAID RAISIN OATMEAL COOKIES

These cookies are made with the ever popular oats and raisin combination. They are good in every way.

    1 cup sugar
    2 cups sifted flour
    1 teaspoon salt
    1 teaspoon soda
    1 teaspoon cinnamon or allspice
    1 teaspoon nutmeg
    2 cups quick-cooking oats
    1 cup **SUN-MAID Seedless Raisins**
    2 eggs

¾ cup oil or melted shortening

½ cup milk

1 teaspoon vanilla

Sift sugar, flour, salt, soda, cinnamon, and nutmeg into bowl. Add oats and raisins. Beat eggs. Add shortening, milk, and vanilla. Add to dry ingredients and beat well. Drop by teaspoonfuls onto greased baking sheet. Bake in moderate oven (350° F) about 15 minutes. Makes about 3 dozen.

OTHER IRRESISTIBLE DESSERTS: PUDDINGS, MOUSSES, AND MORE

NO-BAKE CARAMEL FLAN

This is a great treat any day or night of the week, for any age group.

½ cup sugar

1 package (3 ounces) **JELL-O®** Brand **AMERICANA®** Golden Egg Custard Mix

1 cup half and half or light cream*

1 cup milk*

1 teaspoon vanilla

Melt sugar in heavy skillet over medium heat, stirring constantly, until golden brown. Pour quickly into four 6-ounce custard cups and rotate quickly to coat with syrup on bottoms and halfway up sides. Blend custard mix with half and half, milk, and vanilla in saucepan. Bring quickly to a boil, stirring constantly. (Mixture will be thin.) Pour into syrup-lined cups. Chill at least 2 hours. Unmold into individual dessert dishes. Makes about 2⅓ cups or 4 servings.

*Or use 2 cups milk.

BASIC FRUIT BLOX

Kids love these little snacks they can eat with their fingers. Good for them, too!

3 envelopes **KNOX** Unflavored Gelatine

1½ cups cold fruit juice

1½ cups fruit juice, heated to boiling

2 tablespoons sugar or honey (optional)

In medium bowl, sprinkle unflavored gelatine over cold juice; let stand 1 minute. Add hot juice and stir until gelatine is completely dissolved. Stir in sugar. Pour into 8- or 9-inch baking pan; chill until firm. To serve, cut into 1-inch squares. Makes about 6 dozen blox.

Frozen Fruit Juice Concentrate Variation: Use cold and boiling water in place of juice. Stir in 1 can (6 ounces) frozen fruit juice concentrate.

Note: Do not use fresh or frozen pineapple juice.

COOLING STRAWBERRY MOLD

> 1 package (6 ounces) strawberry gelatin
> 1½ cups boiling water
> 2 cups (about 3 cups whole) fresh strawberry puree*
> ¼ cup sugar
> ½ cup dry **CARNATION** Nonfat Dry Milk
> ½ cup ice water
> 2 tablespoons lemon juice
> Fresh strawberries

*One 16-ounce bag thawed frozen whole unsweetened strawberries may be used to make 2 cups strawberry puree if fresh berries are not available.

Dissolve gelatin in boiling water in large bowl. Stir in strawberry puree and sugar. Chill until consistency of unbeaten egg whites. Combine nonfat dry milk and ice water in small mixer bowl. Beat at high speed until soft peaks form (3 to 4 minutes). Add lemon juice. Continue beating until stiff peaks form (3 to 4 minutes longer). Fold whipped instant milk into strawberry mixture. Spoon into 6-cup mold. Chill 2 to 3 hours. Serve garnished with fresh strawberries. Makes about 6½ cups.

Cooling Cantaloupe Mold: Substitute orange gelatin for strawberry gelatin and use 2 cups (1 medium) pureed ripe cantaloupe instead of strawberries in Cooling Strawberry Mold recipe. Omit sugar. Proceed as above. Garnish with melon balls.

COOKING TIP: CARNATION Nonfat Dry Milk whips like whipping cream. Its unique whip allows you to create these light, fresh salads which are calcium and protein rich and low in calories.

QUICK AND EASY BAKED ALASKA

Surprise your family by serving Baked Alaska. Using KLON-DIKE® Ice Cream Bars simplifies this delicious recipe.

1 layer of poundcake, sponge cake or other (1 to 1½ inches thick)

4 egg whites

⅛ teaspoon salt

½ cup sugar

¼ teaspoon vanilla

3 5-ounce chocolate-covered vanilla **KLONDIKE®** Ice Cream Bars

Cut cake into rectangle, approximately 4 inches by 10 inches. (Cake should extend about ½ inch beyond bars.) Cut a piece of brown paper about 2 inches longer and wider than cake strip. Preheat oven to 500° F. Add salt to egg whites and beat at high speed until soft peaks form. Gradually add sugar, a spoonful at a time, continuing to beat egg whites until meringue holds stiff peaks. Stir in vanilla.

Arrange the hard, frozen KLONDIKE® Ice Cream Bars close together on the cake strip. Quickly spread meringue over entire surface of ice cream bars and cakes sealing down to paper and all around. Swirl top with spoon. In preheated oven, bake dessert about two minutes or until lightly browned. Return to freezer for four hours (or longer). At serving time, lift dessert off paper and onto cold serving platter. Yields 8 to 10 servings. (Halve recipe for 4 to 6 servings.)

ALMOND RAISIN TORTONI

Definitely special! Yet this dessert is very easy to make with
NABISCO® NILLA® Wafers.

48 NILLA® Wafers

2 cups heavy cream

½ cup confectioners' sugar

¼ cup brandy (optional)

½ cup chopped PLANTERS® Slivered
   Almonds, toasted

½ cup raisins

⅓ cup chopped maraschino cherries

6 maraschino cherries, halved

Arrange 4 NILLA® Wafers upright in each of 12 paper-
lined muffin-pan cups. Beat heavy cream with confectioners' sugar until stiff. If desired, gradually beat in
brandy. Fold in PLANTERS® Slivered Almonds, raisins,
and chopped maraschino cherries; spoon into cookie
shells. Garnish each with a halved maraschino cherry.
Freeze 4 hours or until firm. Makes 12 servings.

FROZEN RASPBERRY MOUSSE

You'll enjoy the compliments you get when you serve this elegant and attractive mousse with its distinctive crust made with OREO® Chocolate Sandwich Cookies.

Crust:

   32 OREO® Chocolate Sandwich Cookies

   ¼ cup butter or margarine

Filling:

   1 (10-ounce) package frozen raspberries, thawed, undrained

   ½ cup sugar

   1 tablespoon lemon juice

   ⅛ teaspoon salt

   2 tablespoons kirsch (optional)

   1 cup heavy cream, whipped

   2 egg whites, at room temperature

1. Make Crust: In large plastic bag, using rolling pin, crush 18 OREO Cookies; set aside. In medium saucepan, over low heat, melt butter or margarine; remove from heat; stir in OREO crumbs. Press evenly onto bottom of 9-inch springform pan; stand remaining 14 whole OREO Cookies around sides. Refrigerate while preparing filling.

2. Make Filling: In blender container, combine raspberries, sugar, lemon juice, salt, and, if desired,
kirsch; blend at medium speed about 1 minute. Pour
into large bowl; fold in whipped cream; set aside. In
small bowl, with electric mixer at high speed, beat
egg whites until stiff. Using rubber spatula, fold into
cream mixture.
3. Pour into prepared crust. Freeze until firm, 4 to 6
hours. Makes 8 to 10 servings.

MOUSSE IN A MINUTE

Unexpected guests? Don't worry about what to serve. Here
is a delicious answer. Your family will love it anytime.

> 1 package (4-serving size) **JELL-O®** Brand
> Chocolate, Lemon, Pistachio, or Vanilla
> Flavor Instant Pudding and Pie Filling
>
> 1½ cups milk
>
> 1 cup thawed **BIRDS EYE® COOL
> WHIP®** Non-Dairy Whipped Topping

Prepare pudding mix with milk as directed on package.
Fold in whipped topping and spoon into dessert dishes.
Garnish with additional whipped topping, if desired.
Makes 2⅔ cups or 5 servings.

FRESH FRUIT PARFAITS

Attractive, simple, and wholesome as a dessert or a refreshing
snack.

    3 oranges, peeled and sectioned
    2 bananas, peeled and thinly sliced
    ¼ cup flaked coconut
    1 container (8-ounce) lemon-flavored
       yogurt
   18 OREO® Chocolate Sandwich Cookies,
       crushed
       Mint sprigs

Reserve 8 orange sections and 4 banana slices for garnish. In medium bowl, combine remaining oranges and bananas, coconut and yogurt. In each of 4 parfait glasses, spoon about ¼ cup fruit mixture; top with 2 tablespoons OREO crumbs. Repeat each layer twice, topping last OREO crumb layer with remaining fruit mixture. Garnish each with reserved orange sections, a banana slice, and mint sprig. Makes 4 servings.

BREAD PUDDING

Try this version of an old-time favorite. It will be a success with kids of all ages!

    1 package (3 ounces) JELL-O® Brand
       AMERICANA® Golden Egg Custard Mix
 1¾ cups milk
    2 tablespoons LOG CABIN® Syrup
    1 egg yolk (optional)
    2 bread slices, lightly toasted

Combine custard mix, milk, syrup, and egg yolk in saucepan. Bring quickly to a boil, stirring constantly. (Mixture will be thin.) Remove from heat. Trim crust from toast; cut into ½-inch cubes and place in 1-quart serving dish. Pour hot custard over toast. Sprinkle with nutmeg, if desired. Cool or chill until set. Makes about 2 cups or 4 servings.

PUDDING IN A CLOUD

This attractive dessert is as perfect for an after-school snack for the kids as it is for special dinner parties.

1 container (4 ounces) **BIRDS EYE®** COOL WHIP® Non-Dairy Whipped Topping, thawed

1 package (4-serving size) JELL-O® Brand Instant Pudding and Pie Filling, any flavor

2 cups *cold* milk

2 tablespoons (about 1 ounce) chopped BAKER'S® GERMAN'S® Sweet Chocolate (optional)

Divide whipped topping among 6 dessert glasses, using about ⅓ cup in each. With the back of a spoon, make a depression in the center and spread topping up the sides of the glasses. Prepare pudding mix with milk as directed on package. Fold in chocolate. Spoon pudding mixture into glasses. Chill. Garnish as desired. Makes about 3½ cups or 6 servings.

SUN-MAID RAISIN GRANOLA

This is a tasty treat that the whole family will enjoy.

    2 cups old-fashioned oats
    1 cup shredded coconut
    ½ cup wheat germ
    1½ cups chopped walnuts
    1 teaspoon salt
    1 can (14 ounces) sweetened condensed
        milk
    ¼ cup oil
    1½ cups **SUN-MAID Raisins**

Combine oats, coconut, wheat germ, nuts, and salt in a large bowl. Stir in condensed milk; add oil and mix thoroughly. Spread mixture on shallow baking pan lined with waxed paper. Bake in 300° F oven, stirring occasionally, 1 hour or until golden. Remove from oven and stir in raisins while still warm. Store in a tightly covered container. Makes 8 cups.

SHAPE 'N ROLL CANDY

A versatile, fun candy recipe. Put these treats into lunch boxes, serve at a dinner party, or bring to friends as a hostess gift.

1 6-ounce package SUN-MAID Fruit Bits
1 cup canned chocolate frosting
1 cup coconut
DIAMOND® Walnuts

Combine one 6-ounce package SUN-MAID Fruit Bits with 1 cup *each* canned chocolate frosting and coconut. Chill. Shape into 1-inch balls. Roll or pat on a coating of finely chopped DIAMOND® Walnuts. Makes about 40 candies. Cover and store in refrigerator.

FIVE-MINUTE FUDGE

Prepare everyone's favorite fudge in just five minutes. This recipe is practically failproof. Watch your cooking time and you'll have smooth, creamy, delicious results every time.

2 tablespoons butter
⅔ cup *undiluted* CARNATION Evaporated Milk
1⅔ cups sugar
½ teaspoon salt
2 cups (4 ounces) miniature marshmallows

1½ cups (1½ 6-ounce packages) semi-sweet
chocolate chips

1 teaspoon vanilla

½ cup chopped nuts

Combine butter, evaporated milk, sugar, and salt in saucepan over medium heat, stirring occasionally. Bring to full boil. Cook 4 to 5 minutes, stirring constantly. Remove from heat. Stir in marshmallows, chocolate, vanilla, and nuts. Stir vigorously for 1 minute (until marshmallows melt and blend). Pour into 8-inch square buttered pan. Cool. Cut in squares. Makes 2 pounds.

GRANOLA SNACK BARS

Here is an irresistibly good snack and dessert idea.

½ cup butter or margarine, softened

¾ cup firmly packed brown sugar

⅓ cup corn syrup

1 egg

½ teaspoon vanilla

3½ cups **QUAKER OATS** (Quick or Old
Fashioned, uncooked)

1 6-ounce package (1 cup) semi-sweet
chocolate pieces

Heat oven to 350° F. Generously grease 13 × 9-inch baking pan. In large bowl, beat together butter, sugar and corn syrup until light and fluffy. Blend in egg and vanilla. Add oats and chocolate pieces; mix well. Press firmly into prepared pan. Bake 20 to 23 minutes or until light golden brown. Cool on wire cooling rack. Refrigerate at least one hour; cut into 2 × 1½-inch bars. Makes 32 bars.

Note: When using Old Fashioned Oats, add ¼ cup all-purpose flour to batter.

DESSERT TOPPINGS

CRUNCHY DESSERT TOPPING

Serve this as a delicious topping for yogurt, pudding, fresh fruit, frozen yogurt, or ice cream.

- ½ cup FLEISCHMANN'S Light Corn Oil Spread
- 3 tablespoons firmly packed light brown sugar
- 3 cups **SHREDDED WHEAT TOASTED WHEAT & RAISINS,** coarsely crushed
- ½ cup chopped PLANTERS® Pecans

In large skillet, over medium heat, melt FLEISCH-MANN'S Light Corn Oil Spread; blend in brown sugar

until melted. Reduce heat to low; stir in SHREDDED
WHEAT TOASTED WHEAT & RAISINS and PLANTERS
Pecans until lightly browned, about 7 minutes. Remove
from heat; cool. Store in tightly covered container. Makes
3 cups.

FRAMINGHAM FUDGE SAUCE

Make a lot of this delicious fudge sauce because it is so
versatile and will be very popular in your house.

    5 squares BAKER'S® Unsweetened
      Chocolate

   ¾ cup milk (or 1 cup heavy cream)

1½ cups sugar

   ¼ teaspoon salt

   ¼ cup light corn syrup

   2 tablespoons butter or margarine

   ½ teaspoon cinnamon (optional)

Place chocolate and milk in saucepan over very low heat;
stir constantly until mixture is smooth. Add sugar, salt,
and corn syrup; cook and stir until sugar is completely
dissolved. Remove from heat and stir in butter and cinnamon. Serve warm over cream puffs, ice cream, cake,
pudding, custard, or fruit. Store in refrigerator in covered container and reheat over hot water before serving.
Makes 2½ cups.

COFFEE FUDGE ICING

These simple icing recipes made with **HIGH POINT®** De-caffeinated Coffee will enhance your favorite layer or sheet cake. For the greatest convenience, use atop a prepared cake mix.

1⅔ cups confectioners' sugar

¼ cup butter

2½ tablespoons prepared **HIGH POINT®**
 Decaffeinated Coffee

Heat together the sugar, butter, and coffee until the butter melts. Cool for 5 minutes, then beat well and pour over the cake, smoothing with a palette knife.

MOCHA ICING

¼ cup butter

1⅔ cups confectioners' sugar

¼ cup cocoa powder

 Prepared HIGH POINT® Decaffeinated
 Coffee

Cream the butter, sugar, and cocoa until light and fluffy. Soften with a little coffee and spread over the cake, marking with a fork.

Beverages

TROPICAL STORM

3/4 cup (6-ounce can) chilled, unsweetened
     pineapple juice

  1 egg

1/3 cup dry **CARNATION Nonfat Dry Milk**

  3 tablespoons sugar

  1 teaspoon vanilla

  1 large ripe banana

 12 ice cubes

Place all ingredients in blender container. Cover and
process on high speed until smooth. If desired, garnish
with pineapple chunk and sprig of mint. Makes 3 cups.

COOKING TIP: Combine CARNATION Nonfat Dry Milk with
fresh fruit or juice to create a refreshing blender drink
which has a high concentration of calcium and protein
without unnecessary liquid.

CINNAMONY STRAWBERRY PUNCH

Especially nice to serve this colorful punch at brunches and luncheons. MAGIC MOUNTAIN Herb Tea makes this an easy recipe.

1 package strawberry gelatin (3-ounce size)

3 cups boiling water

8 bags **MAGIC MOUNTAIN®** Sweet Cinnamon Spice Herb Tea

1 small can frozen limeade

3 canfuls cold water

1 quart ginger ale

Dissolve gelatin in boiling water, in bowl or quart jar. Stir or shake to be sure granules are totally dissolved. Drop eight bags Sweet Cinnamon Spice Herb Tea into hot mixture. (Remove tags before adding.) Steep 10 minutes. Remove tea bags. In separate container, dissolve limeade in water. Add gelatin mixture and stir to blend. Chill till ready to serve. To serve: fill punch bowl with ice, or use ice block. To prevent dilution of punch, use ice cubes or ice frozen in milk cartons made of double strength Sweet Cinnamon Spice Herb Tea. Pour punch mixture over ice. Add ginger ale just before serving. Garnish with whole strawberries. Serves 14.

CREOLE PUNCH

A satisfying thirst-quencher and popular crowd-pleaser.

- 1 can (20 ounces) <u>DOLE Chunk Pineapple in Juice</u>
- 1 can (46 ounces) DOLE Pineapple Juice
- 3 cups orange juice
- ½ cup fresh lemon juice
- 1 quart ginger ale
- 1 basket strawberries

  Mint sprigs

Pour pineapple and can juice into square pan or ice cube trays. Freeze. Chill remaining ingredients. In a large punch bowl, combine frozen pineapple chunks, fruit juices, and ginger ale. Wash and remove stems from strawberries. Cut strawberries in half; add to punch along with mint sprigs. Makes 4 quarts.

O.J. AND CINNAMON SMOOTHIE

This great-tasting drink is a delicious alternative to "empty calorie" snacks.

- 1 envelope <u>CARNATION</u> Vanilla Instant Breakfast
- 1 cup cold whole milk

    3 tablespoons thawed frozen orange juice
       concentrate

  1/8 teaspoon ground cinnamon

    6 ice cubes

Place all ingredients in blender container. Cover and process on high speed until well blended. Makes 1 serving (2¼ cups).

STRAWBERRY YOGURT FROST

A refreshing, satisfying drink, perfect for a snack.

    1 envelope **CARNATION** Strawberry
       Instant Breakfast

    1 cup cold whole milk

  1/3 cup strawberry yogurt

    6 ice cubes

Place all ingredients in blender container. Cover and process on high speed until well blended. Makes 1 serving (2½ cups).

OLD-FASHIONED LEMONADE

This is an "oldie but goodie." Try the variations below and you'll love the results.

> 1 bottle (7½ ounces) **MINUTE MAID®** Lemon Juice
> 1 cup sugar
> 6 cups water
> Ice

Mix MINUTE MAID Lemon Juice, sugar, and water in a half-gallon glass or plastic container until sugar is dissolved, then add ice to fill.

For a Picnic: Carry sugar to the picnic site in a half-gallon glass or plastic container with a tight cover. When ready to serve, add lemon juice and water, cover tightly, and shake to dissolve sugar, then fill container with ice.

Lemonade Olé: Use 2 cups of sangria instead of 2 cups of the water; proceed as above.

Better Berry Lemonade: Add one 10-ounce package frozen sweetened strawberries to the lemon juice, sugar, and water, and mix thoroughly. Add ice to chill, and perhaps a little more water, according to your taste.

PEACHY YOGURT SHAKE

Here is a refreshing and filling snack that is nutritious and delicious. DEL MONTE Lite Fruits help keep the calories down.

1 cup plain yogurt

1 can (8½ ounces) **DEL MONTE** Lite

Yellow Cling Sliced Peaches

4 ice cubes

2 to 3 drops almond extract

Combine ingredients in blender container. Cover; blend until smooth. Pour into 2 glasses and sprinkle with cinnamon, if desired. Makes 2 servings (8 ounces each).

PRUNE SHAKE

This shake is delicious and wholesome.

½ cup chilled **SUNSWEET** Prune Juice

1 cup vanilla ice cream

Measure prune juice and ice cream into blender jar. Cover and blend smooth. Pour into a 12-ounce glass. Makes 1 serving (about 1¼ cups).

Chocolate Shake: Use chocolate ice cream instead of vanilla, and flavor to taste with unsweetened chocolate extract.

VIENNESE SPICED COFFEE

Indulge yourself with this fantastic coffee treat. Serve it to special guests, too.

3 cups hot Instant **HIGH POINT**® Decaffeinated Coffee

3 tablespoons sugar

8 whole cloves

3 inches stick cinnamon

Whipped cream

Cinnamon sticks

Orange slices, quartered, or

finely shredded orange peel

In saucepan, combine hot coffee, sugar, cloves, and the 3 inches stick cinnamon. Cover; bring mixture to boiling. Remove from heat, cover, and let stand 5 minutes. Strain; discard spices.

Pour hot coffee into cups or heatproof glasses; top each with a dollop of whipped cream. Serve with cinnamon stick stirrers. Garnish with quartered orange slices or shredded orange peel. Serve immediately. Makes 4 to 6 servings.

Cooking and Shopping Tips

COOKING TIPS

To get more juice from a citrus fruit (1) roll repeatedly on a hard surface or (2) allow to warm to room temperature before squeezing or (3) put into warm water.

To prevent chopped onions from discoloring when serving raw, place in a strainer and toss them under cold running water.

Salting foods: Salt draws moisture out of vegetables, as it does with meats. Salting cucumbers makes them look limp, but it keeps them crunchy for days.

Making crepes: The temperature of the pan is vital. To test for the proper temperature, as the pan is preheating over medium heat, sprinkle a few drops of water in the pan. If the drops sizzle and bounce, the pan is at the right temperature to begin pouring on batter.

When cooking crepes, brown them on one side only. When done, the tops will look dry and the edges will curl. This takes about 50 seconds.

Pork must be well cooked to prevent disease.

Whipping cream must be at least a day old. Bowl, beaters, and cream should all be well chilled before beating. Be careful not to overbeat. Beat until glossy peaks form.

Whipping cream should expand to twice its volume.

Garlic: To peel, crush, or chop garlic, separate cloves from the garlic head by placing head on its side and hitting with palm of hand.

Do not store thin fish fillets in freezer for a long time. They get freezer burn easily.

General baking hint: Ingredients should be at room temperature for best results.

Do not open oven door during first half of time any cake is baking. This can cause it to fall.

Press a finger lightly on the cake's surface to see if it is finished. It should spring back and leave no imprint.

Freezing cheese: To freeze cheese, wrap tightly with freezer wrap. Thaw cheese slowly in the refrigerator to minimize crumbling.

Avoid flour lumping by adding over half of the liquid to the mixture so that it's thick, and mix until no dry flour is left. Then add the rest of the liquid.

When green peppers are allowed to ripen fully, they turn brilliant red.

A small amount of lemon juice poured over fruit prevents it from turning brown and can enhance the flavor.

If too much salt is added to stew or soup, add a raw potato, sliced, to absorb salt during cooking.

Add a few teaspoons of cooking oil to the water when cooking rice, noodles, or spaghetti to prevent sticking together and boiling over.

Basic principles
for using eggs:

When cooking, use a moderate to low temperature with exact timing.

Egg whites freeze well in tightly closed jar and can be defrosted and refrozen.

Egg yolks can be frozen but don't soften completely when thawed.

Beaten egg whites will be more stable if you add one teaspoon of cream of tartar for about seven egg whites. Lemon juice works similarly.

Egg whites will not beat well if any yolk is present.

Beat egg whites until stiff and glistening but not dry. Do not use a blender. Use mixer or whisk.

When making meringues, add sugar gradually to beaten egg whites to increase the stability of the foam. Added sugar prevents decreasing the volume.

Eggs are easiest to separate when cold, but whites reach their fullest volume if allowed to warm to room temperature.

When egg yolks are added to hot mixtures all at once, they may begin to coagulate too rapidly and form lumps. Therefore, pour small amounts of the hot mixture into the yolks to warm them and then stir the warmed egg-yolk mixture into the remaining hot mixture.

For stirred custard mixtures, the eggs are cooked to the proper doneness when a thin film coats or adheres to a metal spoon dipped into the custard.

It is the air beaten into egg whites that expands as a soufflé bakes which gives it impressive height.

To beat egg whites and get greatest volume, the eggs should be fresh and at room temperature.

To peel hard-cooked eggs easily, place eggs under cold running water until they are cooled.

SHOPPING TIPS

Use coupons when you shop and you can save a lot of money. Shop in stores that offer double value for your coupons. (Some stores offer triple value.)

The following is a list of qualities and characteristics that you should look for in order to select the best food buys.

Buying Meats, Fish, Poultry

Beef: Fine grained, firm, and bright red color. Vacuum-packed beef has a purplish-red color.

Lamb: Fine grained and pinkish-red in color. Older lamb, called mutton, is darker colored, and coarser.

Veal: Fine grained, velvety in texture, light grayish-pink in color, and very lean.

Pork: Firm, fine grained, grayish-pink, for fresh pork. Look for delicate rose color for cured pork.

Fish: Selecting whole fresh fish—look for bright, clear eyes, firm, springy flesh, and fresh odor or none. Selecting frozen fish—it should be frozen solid, not discolored, have no odor. *Note:* The best test for selecting fish is to smell it. Very fresh fish has no smell.

Poultry: Make sure skin is not dry, not hard, not bruised. If buying frozen poultry, inspect for "freezer burn," i.e., brownish skin areas.

Buying Fruit

In general, fruits should be unblemished and have vivid coloration, characteristic of that fruit.

Peaches: Should not have any green tinge.

Berries: Firm; avoid if mold or wetness present.

Watermelons: Whole watermelons should have some creamy area on outer shell. Cut melons should have bright red fruit.

Citrus: Heavy for size.

Buying Vegetables

Artichokes: Choose artichokes with tight, compact heads. Without open or curled leaves on sides.

Asparagus: Tightly closed, compact tips and firm, brittle stalks that are green almost entire length.

Beans: Green small, crisp, bright green beans.

Bean pods: Bright in appearance, free of blemish, and firm.

Dried beans: Bright, uniform color. Mixed sizes will cause uneven cooking.

Bean sprouts: Crisp, white with beans attached.

Beets: Small, firm, smooth skinned, crisp tops.

Broccoli: Compact, tightly closed dark-green flowerets. Avoid yellowing buds. Stalks firm and tender.

Brussels sprouts: Compact bright green in color and free from blemishes. Avoid wilted leaves.

Cabbage: Green or red—fresh, firm, heavy heads for their size. Outer leaves blemish-free.

Carrots: Firm, bright, well shaped.

Cauliflower: Firm, compact, creamy white head.

Celery: Rigid, crisp, green stalks.

Collards: Green, tender, unblemished leaves.

Corn: Green husks; silk ends that are free from decay; plump, milky kernels inside.

Cucumber: Firm, well shaped.

Eggplant: Firm, shiny, heavy for size. Purple uniformly smooth skin.

Lettuce: Unwilted, crisp, deep color, fresh looking.

Mushrooms: Smooth and plump. Avoid wilted or slick.

Onions: Firm, dry, no green sprouts.

Onions, green or scallions: Crisp, bright green tops.

Parsnips: Smooth, firm, well shaped roots.

Peas: Choose well filled, bright, green, fresh, crisp.

Peppers: Glossy, firm.

Potatoes: Firm, smooth skins, with no sprouts or blemishes or black spots or green areas.

Sweet Potatoes: Dry yellow flesh. Yams: Deeper yellow than sweet potatoes and more moist than sweet potatoes. Color is not important; look for thick, medium-sized potatoes that taper at the ends.

Rutabaga: Heavy for their size, firm, and have generally smooth round or elongated shape.

Spinach: Crisp, tender, deep green unwilted leaves.

Summer squash: Firm,smooth, glossy, heavy.

Tomatoes: Smooth, well formed, firm, not hard.

IMPORTANT CULINARY DEFINITIONS

Al dente (Italian)—Describes the degree (barely tender) to which food should be cooked.

Antipasto (Italian)—Hot or cold appetizer, assortment of vegetables, meat, and/or fish.

Aspic—A flavored glaze from meat, fish, or poultry, or a molded salad made from vegetables or meat stock.

Au gratin—Food topped with bread crumbs and/or grated cheese and broiled or baked until brown.

Au jus (French)—Served in natural juice or gravy.

Baste—Brush or spoon liquid or fat over food to keep moist while cooking.

Beat—To make a mixture smooth and add air with brisk motion.

Blend—To combine two or more ingredients and mix together until smooth and uniform.

Bisque—Thick cream soup, usually made from pureed vegetables or fish.

Blanch—To boil briefly in water or steam in order to remove skin, to whiten, or to cook partially.

Boil—To cook liquid to 212° F (or 100° C) at sea level.

Boil gently—Bubbles just begin to break the surface. **Full rolling boil**—There is rapid bubbling, throughout the liquid, which does not stop when stirred.

Braise—Cook slowly in a small amount of liquid in a covered pan.

Bread—To coat with crumbs.

Brown—To cook food until browned, turning until all sides are browned.

Caramelize—To cook sugar over low heat, while stirring, until it forms a golden-brown syrup.

Cream—To beat a mixture until it becomes smooth and fluffy.

Cube—Cut into pieces that are the same size on each side—at least ½ inch.

Cut in—To incorporate a solid fat into a flour mixture, using a pastry blender or two knives used scissor-fashion.

Dal—The Indian name for legumes.

Deep-fry—To cook in hot fat deep enough to allow the food to float.

Dice—Cut into cubes that are ⅛ to ¼ inch on each side.

Dissolve—Stir a dry ingredient into a liquid until the dry ingredient is no longer visible.

Dredge—Sprinkle food lightly with flour or other dry ingredient until coated.

En brochette (French)—Food cooked on skewers.

Fillet—To remove all bones.

Flake—Gently break into small pieces.

Fold in—To combine delicate ingredients with another mixture using gentle circular motions to prevent loss of air.

Fry—To cook food in hot fat.

Glaze—Brush moisture on a food to give a glossy appearance or a hard finish. Usually the glaze adds flavor.

Grate—To rub food on a grater, or to use a blender or a food processor to produce fine particles.

Grind—To cut food into fine particles, using a food grinder, a blender, or a food processor.

Knead—To work dough with the heel of the hand in a pressing, rolling, and folding motion on a floured surface.

Marinate—Allow a food to stand in a liquid that adds flavor to the food.

Meringue—Stiffly beaten egg whites with sugar gradually beaten in until it is dissolved.

Mince—To cut or chop into very fine pieces.

Mix—Combine ingredients by stirring.

Parboil—To cook foods partially in a liquid.

Partially set—To chill a gelatin mixture to the point in setting when it has consistency of raw egg whites.

Poach—To cook food over low heat in liquid.

Puree—Use a blender, food processor, or food mill to convert a food into a liquid or heavy paste.

Render—To melt solid fat away from other tissue.

Sauté—Cook in a small amount of fat.

Scald—To heat just under the boiling point, that is, until tiny bubbles begin to form on the sides of pot.

Score—Cut shallow grooves or slits through the outer layer of a food.

Sear—To brown surface of food over high heat.

Simmer—To cook just below the boiling point over low heat.

Steep—Extract the flavor or color from a substance by letting it stand in hot liquid.

Stir-fry—To cook food quickly by stirring constantly in a small amount of hot fat.

Toss—To mix lightly.

Truss—To secure so that something holds its shape in cooking.

Whip—Beat food to increase volume by incorporating air.

HOW TO SUBSTITUTE ONE INGREDIENT FOR ANOTHER IN AN EMERGENCY

Instead of	Amount	Use This
Buttermilk	1 cup	1 cup plain yogurt
Cream, light	1 cup	2 tablespoons butter plus 1 cup minus 2 tablespoons
Cream, sour	1 cup	3 tablespoons butter plus $7/8$ cup yogurt
Cream of tartar		lemon juice

Instead of	Amount	Use This
Cream, whipping	1 cup	2 cups whipped cream or 2 cups dessert topping
Corn syrup	1 cup	1 cup granulated sugar plus ¼ cup liquid
Egg for cooking	1 whole	2 egg whites
Egg for baking	1 whole	½ teaspoon baking powder plus 2 tablespoons soy flour
Flour for thickening	1 tablespoon flour	½ teaspoon corn starch or 1½ tablespoons quick-cooking tapioca
Garlic	1 clove	⅛ teaspoon garlic powder or 1 tablespoon minced dried garlic
Ginger	1 tablespoon	⅛ teaspoon powdered ginger
Honey	1 cup	1¼ cups sugar plus ¼ cup liquid
Horseradish	1 tablespoon fresh, grated	1 tablespoon bottled horseradish
Lemon	1 whole	2 or 3 tablespoons lemon juice or 1½ teaspoons grated lemon rind

Instead of	Amount	Use This
	1 teaspoon juice	½ teaspoon vinegar
	1 teaspoon shredded rind	½ teaspoon lemon extract
Lime	1 whole	1½ tablespoons lime juice
Mushrooms	1 pound	6 oz. canned mushrooms
Mustard	1 teaspoon dry or powdered	1 tablespoon prepared mustard
Orange	1 medium	7 tablespoons orange juice
Saccharin	¼ grain	1 teaspoon sugar
Tomato sauce	2 cups	¾ cup tomato paste plus 1 cup water
Yogurt	1 cup	1 cup buttermilk

COMMON FOOD EQUIVALENTS

Bread crumbs	3 oz.	1 cup
Butter or margarine	1 lb.	2 cups
Butter	¼ lb.	8 tablespoons or ½ cup
Cheese	1 lb.	4 cups, grated

Chocolate	1 oz.	1 square
Coconut, shred-ded	7 oz.	2⅔ cups, loosely packed
Cottage cheese	1 lb.	2 cups
Cranberries	1 lb.	4 cups
Cream cheese	3-oz. package	6⅔ tablespoons
Cream of tartar	1 oz.	3 tablespoons
Eggs, whole	4–6	1 cup
Flour, all-pur-pose	1 lb.	4 cups, unsifted
Flour, cake	1 lb.	4½ cups, un-sifted
Honey	12 oz.	1 cup
Lemon juice	1 lemon	2 to 3 table-spoons
Onions	1 medium	½ cup, chopped
Raisins	1 lb.	3 cups
Rice, uncooked	1 cup	3 cups, cooked
Spinach	1 lb.	2 cups, cooked
Sugar, brown	1 lb.	2½ cups, firmly packed
Sugar, confec-tioners'	1 lb.	4 cups
Sugar, granu-lated	1 lb.	2 cups
Whipping cream	1 cup	2 cups, whipped

COOKING MEASUREMENTS

Dash = less than ⅛ teaspoon

3 teaspoons = 1 tablespoon

2 liquid tablespoons = 1 ounce

16 tablespoons = 1 cup

1 cup = ½ pint (8 ounces)

4 cups = 2 pints = 1 quart = 32 ounces

1 liquid cup = 1 pound = 16 ounces

4 quarts = 1 gallon = 64 ounces

TEMPERATURE GUIDE

Very slow oven	225° F
Slow oven	250° F to 300° F
Moderate oven	325° F to 375° F
Hot oven	400° F to 450° F
Very hot oven	475° F and over

General Index

Recipe Index

List of Coupons

ABOUT THE AUTHOR

Marion Joyce is the author of the column "The Coupon Cookbook Corner," which appears weekly in over 400 newspapers nationwide. She is also hostess for *The Coupon Cookbook* television show, which features cooking demonstrations and is being syndicated nationally. She currently resides in Scarsdale in Westchester County, New York.

SAVE MONEY

WITH THESE

VALUABLE COUPONS

25¢

25¢

199

SAVE MONEY

WITH THESE

VALUABLE COUPONS

25¢ **25¢**

SAVE 25¢
ON ONE BOTTLE OF 10 OR 15 OZ. SIZE
OR TWO 5 OZ. SIZE BOTTLES OF
A.1. STEAK SAUCE

TO RETAILER: Heublein, Inc. will redeem this coupon for face value plus 7¢ if you receive it on sale of product indicated. Coupon may not be assigned or transferred. Invoices proving purchase of sufficient stock to cover coupons must be submitted on request. Customer must pay sales tax. Void where prohibited, taxed or restricted by law. Cash value 1/20¢. For redemption mail to Heublein, Inc., P.O. Box 1038, Clinton Iowa 52734.

54400 200884

STORE COUPON

25¢ **25¢**

STORE COUPON

SAVE 15¢
ON **ARGO** OR **KINGSFORD'S**
CORN STARCH

THICKENS SAUCES, GRAVIES & DESSERTS

NO EXPIRATION DATE

DEALER: This coupon will be redeemed for face value plus 8¢ handling if used in accordance with the offer stated hereon; any other use, including reproduction, constitutes fraud. Limit one coupon per transaction. Coupon not transferable. Void where prohibited, taxed, or otherwise restricted. Proof of purchase of sufficient merchandise to cover coupons submitted must be shown on request. Cash redemption value 1/20¢. Customer must pay any sales tax. Good only in U.S.A. Send to: Best Foods, Box 102, Clinton, Iowa 52734.

203

10¢ **10¢**

10¢ **10¢**

20¢ **20¢**

50000 124078

20¢ **20¢**

20¢ **20¢**

20¢ **20¢**

SAVE 25¢
ON 2 CUPS DANNON YOGURT

25¢

99972 126892

25¢ (top right)

COUPON

COUPON

STORE COUPON

10¢

SAVE 10¢
on the purchase of any Del Monte® Fruits

Regular or Lite

24000 155937

10¢

STORE COUPON

10¢

SAVE 10¢
on the purchase of any Del Monte® Vegetables

Regular or No Salt Added

24000 155390

10¢

No matter what you cook…

DOLE® SUITS YOUR STYLE!

SAVE 20¢

on TWO 20-oz. cans
of Dole® Pineapple—
any style.

20¢ **20¢**
20¢ **20¢**

STORE COUPON

MANUFACTURER'S COUPON/NO EXPIRATION DATE

SAVE 20¢

20¢

WHEN YOU BUY DREAM WHIP® BRAND WHIPPED TOPPING MIX

20¢

LIMIT—ONE COUPON PER PURCHASE

GENERAL FOODS CORPORATION

CCB40065

NABISCO

SAVE 25¢

25¢

on any purchase of
FIG NEWTONS®
Cookies

STORE COUPON

STORE COUPON

FIG NEWTONS…
the fruit chewy cookie.

44000 111276

25¢

McG   /Spring/84

213

SAVE 20¢

when you buy TWO 20-oz. cans of Dole® Pineapple (any style).

20¢ 20¢ 20¢

RETAILER: For each coupon you accept as our authorized agent, we will pay you the face value of this coupon plus 7¢ handling, provided you and your customers have complied with the terms of this offer. Any other application constitutes fraud. Invoices showing purchase of sufficient stock to cover all coupons redeemed must be shown on request. Void if redeemed by other than retail customer, if prohibited, taxed or restricted. Customer must pay sales tax. Cash value 1/20 of 1¢. You may redeem by mailing to: DOLE,® P.O. Box 1420, Clinton, Iowa 52734. One coupon per purchase. Good only in U.S.A.
No expiration date.

38900 103185

STORE COUPON

MANUFACTURER'S COUPON/NO EXPIRATION DATE

SAVE 20¢

WHEN YOU BUY DREAM WHIP® BRAND WHIPPED TOPPING MIX

20¢

To the retailer: General Foods Corp. will reimburse you for the face value of this coupon plus 8¢ for handling if you receive it on the sale of the specified product and if upon request you submit evidence of purchase thereof satisfactory to General Foods Corp. Coupon may not be assigned, transferred or reproduced. Customer must pay any sales tax. Void where prohibited, taxed or restricted by law. Good only in U.S.A., Puerto Rico and U.S. Gov't. install. Cash value: 1/20¢. Coupon will not be honored if presented through outside agencies, brokers or others who are not retail distributors of our merchandise or specifically authorized by us to present coupons for redemption. For redemption of properly received and handled coupon, mail to General Foods Corp., P.O. Box 103, Kankakee, IL 06092

This coupon good only on purchase of product indicated.
Any other use constitutes fraud.

LIMIT—ONE COUPON PER PURCHASE

20¢

GENERAL FOODS CORPORATION

CCB40065

25¢ 25¢

SAVE 25¢
on any purchase of FIG NEWTONS® Cookies

STORE COUPON

STORE COUPON

TO THE RETAILER: Coupon will be redeemed for 25¢ plus 8¢ for handling when you comply with offer terms. Any other application constitutes fraud. Invoices proving sufficient purchases of this product to cover coupons presented must be available on request. Consumer to pay applicable sales tax. Coupon may not be assigned or transferred by you. Coupon void when presented by outside agency or broker or where use is prohibited, restricted or taxed. Good only in U.S.A. Cash value 1/20¢. Mail to NABISCO BRANDS, INC., P.O. Box 1754, Clinton, Iowa 52734. Only one coupon redeemed per purchase.

44000 111276

25¢

HERE'S 20¢ TO TRY ONE OF FRENCH'S EXTRA CREAMY, EXTRA TASTY POTATOES

20¢ **20¢**

Mr Grocer The R T French Company will redeem this coupon for 20¢ plus 7¢ handling if you receive it on the sale of French's Tangy Au Gratin or Cheese Scalloped or Pancake Mix or Sour Cream & Chives or Crispy Top Scalloped Any other application constitutes fraud Invoices showing your purchases of sufficient stock to cover all coupons redeemed must be shown upon request Coupons may not be assigned or transferred Void where prohibited taxed or restricted by law Cash value 1/20 of 1¢ Customer pays any sales tax For redemption of properly received and handled coupons mail to The R T French Company P O Box 1345 Clinton Iowa 52734 OFFER LIMITED TO ONE COUPON PER PURCHASE

STORE COUPON   41500 130319

20¢ **20¢**

41500 130319

50¢ off

...the finest dessert toppings, brandied fruits, relishes and condiments... since 1888

Available at specialty food shops, and in department stores and supermarket fancy food sections.

This coupon good only on the product specified. Any other application constitutes fraud. Coupon is void where taxed, restricted or prohibited by law. Cash value 1/20 of one cent. Mail coupon to: **Iroquois Grocery Products, P.O. Box 1542, Clinton, Iowa 52734.**

50¢ off   18600 100871

STORE COUPON   10¢

240881

DEALER: Send this coupon after redemption to H.J. Heinz Company, P.O. Box 1685, Elm City, NC 27898 for reimbursement of 10¢ plus 8¢ handling. Invoices proving purchase of sufficient stock of Heinz Chili Sauce to cover coupons presented must be shown upon request. Failure to do so will void all coupons. Coupons nontransferable. Sales tax must be paid by customer. Void wherever prohibited, taxed or restricted. **GOOD ONLY ON HEINZ CHILI SAUCE. ANY OTHER USE CONSTITUTES FRAUD.**

OFFER LIMITED TO ONE COUPON PER PURCHASE.

Heinz

Printed in U.S.A.   ©1983 H.J. Heinz Co.   240881

10¢

219

SAVE 50¢ when you buy

ONE 8 oz. or ONE 4 oz. or TWO 2 oz. Jars of Instant

HIGH POINT®

DECAFFEINATED COFFEE ©P

40588

221

The Original...always the best.

Christian Isaly came to America from Switzerland 150 years ago, with a century of family secrets for making delicious Swiss dairy products. By 1900, his grandson, William, had earned a reputation for making the finest dairy and ice cream products.

After seeking to create a superior ice cream treat for many years, they discovered that dipping their special, creamy vanilla ice cream twice in Swiss milk chocolate made a unique and delicious ice cream bar that everyone loved. When a friend remarked that this new product was "as good as gold", the Isaly family named it "Klondike". To this day, the Klondike name is the symbol of the very best ice cream bars.

Klondikes are still made from Sam Isaly's original recipe. We know you'll agree that they are specially delicious.

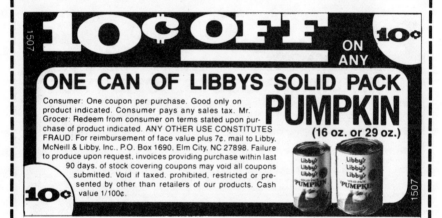

226

227

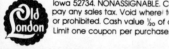

231

232

234

236

10¢   SAVE 10¢   10¢
ON SUN-MAID® APRICOTS.

RETAILER: This coupon is redeemable for face value and 8¢ handling charges provided as follows: it is received on a retail sale of the product specified herein. You may mail it to Sun-Diamond Growers of California, P.O. Box 1404, Clinton, Iowa 52734. On request, you must supply invoices proving sufficient stock purchases covering coupons submitted for redemption. Other use constitutes fraud. Coupon may not be assigned or transferred. Customer must pay any sales tax. Void where prohibited, taxed, license required or restricted by law. Cash value 1/20¢. Good only in U.S.A. Offer limited to one coupon per purchase.

41143 105918

© Sun-Diamond Growers of California, 1983.

10¢   SAVE 10¢   10¢
ON SUN-MAID® FRUIT BITS.

RETAILER: This coupon is redeemable for face value and 7¢ handling charges provided as follows: it is received on a retail sale of the product specified herein. You may mail it to Sun-Diamond Growers of California, P.O. Box 1404, Clinton, Iowa 52734. On request, you must supply invoices proving sufficient stock purchases covering coupons submitted for redemption. Other use constitutes fraud. Coupon may not be assigned or transferred. Customer must pay any sales tax. Void where prohibited, taxed, license required or restricted by law. Cash value 1/20¢. Good only in U.S.A. Offer limited to one coupon per purchase.

41143 105686

© Sun-Diamond Growers of California, 1983.

10¢   SUN-MAID.®   10¢
AMERICA'S FAVORITE RAISIN
SAVE 10¢ ON ANY SIZE PACKAGE OF SUN-MAID RAISINS

RETAILER: This coupon is redeemable for face value and 7¢ handling charges provided as follows: it is received on a retail sale of the product specified herein. You mail it to Sun-Diamond Growers of California, P.O. Box 1404, Clinton, Iowa 52734. On request, you must supply invoices proving sufficient stock purchases covering coupons submitted for redemption. Other use constitutes fraud. Coupon may not be assigned or transferred. Customer must pay any sales tax. Void where prohibited, taxed, license required or restricted by law. Cash value 1/20¢. Good only in U.S.A. Offer limited to one coupon per purchase.

41143 105884

© Sun-Diamond Growers of California, 1983.

10¢   SAVE 10¢   10¢
ON SUN-MAID® APRICOTS.

RETAILER: This coupon is redeemable for face value and 8¢ handling charges provided as follows: it is received on a retail sale of the product specified herein. You may mail it to Sun-Diamond Growers of California, P.O. Box 1404, Clinton, Iowa 52734. On request, you must supply invoices proving sufficient stock purchases covering coupons submitted for redemption. Other use constitutes fraud. Coupon may not be assigned or transferred. Customer must pay any sales tax. Void where prohibited, taxed, license required or restricted by law. Cash value 1/20¢. Good only in U.S.A. Offer limited to one coupon per purchase.

41143 105918

© Sun-Diamond Growers of California, 1983.

10¢   SAVE 10¢   10¢
ON SUN-MAID® FRUIT BITS.

RETAILER: This coupon is redeemable for face value and 7¢ handling charges provided as follows: it is received on a retail sale of the product specified herein. You may mail it to Sun-Diamond Growers of California, P.O. Box 1404, Clinton, Iowa 52734. On request, you must supply invoices proving sufficient stock purchases covering coupons submitted for redemption. Other use constitutes fraud. Coupon may not be assigned or transferred. Customer must pay any sales tax. Void where prohibited, taxed, license required or restricted by law. Cash value 1/20¢. Good only in U.S.A. Offer limited to one coupon per purchase.

41143 105686

© Sun-Diamond Growers of California, 1983.

10¢   SUN-MAID.®   10¢
AMERICA'S FAVORITE RAISIN
SAVE 10¢ ON ANY SIZE PACKAGE OF SUN-MAID RAISINS

RETAILER: This coupon is redeemable for face value and 7¢ handling charges provided as follows: it is received on a retail sale of the product specified herein. You mail it to Sun-Diamond Growers of California, P.O. Box 1404, Clinton, Iowa 52734. On request, you must supply invoices proving sufficient stock purchases covering coupons submitted for redemption. Other use constitutes fraud. Coupon may not be assigned or transferred. Customer must pay any sales tax. Void where prohibited, taxed, license required or restricted by law. Cash value 1/20¢. Good only in U.S.A. Offer limited to one coupon per purchase.

41143 105884

© Sun-Diamond Growers of California, 1983.

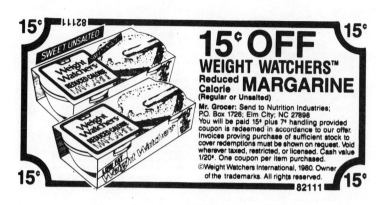

15¢ OFF
15¢ · 15¢

82111

SWEET UNSALTED

WEIGHT WATCHERS™
Reduced **MARGARINE**
Calorie
(Regular or Unsalted)

15¢ · 15¢
82111

15¢ OFF
15¢ · 15¢

82413

ON WEIGHT WATCHERS™
Reduced **MAYONNAISE**
Calorie

15¢ · 15¢
82413

save 20¢

on any variety of

WHEATSWORTH®
STONE GROUND WHEAT CRACKERS

STORE COUPON

243

15¢ OFF

15¢   15¢

WEIGHT WATCHERS™
Reduced **MARGARINE**
Calorie
(Regular or Unsalted)

SWEET UNSALTED

Mr. Grocer: Send to Nutrition Industries;
P.O. Box 1726; Elm City; NC 27898
You will be paid 15¢ plus 7¢ handling provided
coupon is redeemed in accordance to our offer.
Invoices proving purchase of sufficient stock to
cover redemptions must be shown on request. Void
wherever taxed, restricted, or licensed. Cash value
1/20¢. One coupon per item purchased.
©Weight Watchers International, 1980. Owner
of the trademarks. All rights reserved.

15¢   15¢

82111

15¢ OFF

15¢   15¢

ON WEIGHT WATCHERS™
Reduced **MAYONNAISE**
Calorie

Weight Watchers
REDUCED CALORIE MAYONNAISE

Mr. Grocer: Send to Nutrition Industries;
P.O. Box 1726; Elm City; NC 27898
You will be paid 15¢ plus 7¢ handling provided
coupon is redeemed in accordance to our offer.
Invoices proving purchase of sufficient stock to
cover redemptions must be shown on request. Void
wherever taxed, restricted, or licensed. Cash value
1/20¢. One coupon per item purchased.
©Weight Watchers International, 1980.
Owner of the trademarks. All rights reserved.

15¢   15¢

82413

---

save 20¢ on any variety of
WHEATSWORTH
STONE GROUND WHEAT CRACKERS

TO THE RETAILER: We will redeem this coupon for 20¢ plus 8¢ for handling when the terms of this offer
have been complied with. Any other application constitutes fraud. Invoices proving sufficient purchase to
cover coupons redeemed must be available upon request. Consumer to pay sales tax where applicable.
Coupon may not be assigned or transferred by you. Coupon void when presented to outside agency or
where its use is prohibited, restricted or taxed. Cash value 1/20¢ of 1¢ • Retailer Mail to: NABISCO
BRANDS, INC., P.O. Box 1754, Clinton, Iowa 52734
© 1983 NABISCO BRANDS, INC.

NABISCO
BRANDS   STORE COUPON   44000 111656
    McG   /Spring/84